City Teachers

City Teachers

TEACHING AND SCHOOL REFORM
IN HISTORICAL PERSPECTIVE

Kate Rousmaniere

Teachers College, Columbia University
New York and London

Published by Teachers College Press, 1234 Amsterdam Avenue, New York, NY 10027

Library of Congress Cataloging-in-Publication Data

Rousmaniere, Kate, 1958–
    City teachers : teaching and school reform in historical
 perspective / Kate Rousmaniere.
        p.   cm.
     Includes bibliographical references (p.   ) and index.
      ISBN 0-8077-3589-2 (cloth : alk. paper).—ISBN 0-8077-3588-4
 (pbk. : alk. paper)
        1. Teachers—New York (State)—New York—History—20th century.
 2. Teachers—New York (State)—New York—Political activity—
 History—20th century.   3. School management and organization—New
 York (State)—New York—History—20th century.   I. Title.
 LB1775.3.N7R68   1997
 371.1′009747′109042—dc20   96-43883

ISBN 0-8077-3588-4 (paper)
ISBN 0-8077-3589-2 (cloth)

Printed on acid-free paper
Manufactured in the United States of America

04 03 02 01 00 99 98 97   8 7 6 5 4 3 2 1

Contents

Acknowledgments

THIS STUDY IS BASED upon and driven by the testimony of 21 retired teachers, contacted through the New York City Retired Teachers Association, who generously offered to share with a stranger their accounts of their experiences as city teachers in the 1920s. I am especially indebted to my friend Isabel Ross, a 40-year career teacher in Brooklyn's elementary and junior high schools, and 98 years old at this writing.

My interest in the history of teachers' work originated in my own tenure as a high school teacher, during which time I observed the dismantling of a richly collective teachers' work culture by school administrators who interpreted teachers' occupational pride as dangerous worker insubordination. My vision of that fleeting moment of teacher collegiality, and the tradition of teacher independence at that school has inspired this historical study of teachers' responses to their working conditions. Conversations with current and former classroom teachers from that school and other schools have deepened my understanding of the complexity and vivacity of teachers' daily work. I am particularly appreciative of the personal and political insights of Paula Titon, who taught me both how to teach social studies and how to be a teacher, and for the hours of conversation about teaching spent with Michele Reich, Louise Gibson, Joan Scott, Jennifer Hall, Peggy McIntosh, Gabrielle Keller, and Phyllis Scattergood.

In the early stages of my research and writing, Ellen Condliffe Lagemann and the late Lawrence Cremin provided perceptive guidance and a challenging academic climate at Teachers College. Josh Freeman and Betsy Blackmar helped me conceptualize the link between educational history and labor history. The bulk of the research was conducted in the Special Collections Department of Teachers College's Milbank Memorial Library, where David Ment provided both the archival materials and the animated and generous work culture that made the experience meaningful, productive, and fun. As graduate students, Dan Humphrey and I collaborated in the writing and criticisms of each other's dissertations on a daily basis for three years.

That cooperative relationship provided depth and relevance to both of our projects, and to our critical thinking about American education.

The Department of Educational Leadership at Miami University provided both financial support and a dynamic collegial community to strengthen and clarify my earlier ideas. In multiple conversations about teaching, research, writing, and work, Richard Quantz, Bernard Badiali, and Marcia Baxter Magolda have enhanced this study. I am grateful also for funding from the School of Education and Allied Professions at Miami University and the Oberlin College Alumni Fellowship.

Members of the AERA Special Interest Group, Teachers' Work/Teachers' Unions have created a rich community of interdisciplinary and international scholars focusing on the politics and culture of teachers' work. In particular, Harry Smaller, Martin Lawn, Wayne Urban, Richard Altenbaugh, Joe Newman, and Sara Freedman have by their own research and collegiality encouraged this and other studies on the labor process of teaching. Colleagues and friends across disciplines have read sections of this manuscript and provided the conversations and questions that helped it to crystallize. Kari Dehli, Martin Lawn, Wayne Urban, Richard Quantz, Mary Kupiec Cayton, Gretchen Townsend, Barry Franklin, and Frances Fowler have generously contributed their time and thought to this project. Sharon Lane and Louisa Campbell conducted critical last-minute research. As this book emerged into its final shape, I was lucky to find Elliott Gorn, who walked and talked me through this and almost everything else in my path.

My uncle, Albert H. Gordon, provided the resources to allow me to follow my interest in the historical development of schools and teachers. His unconditional faith in my potential, and in the potential of all learning endeavors, fueled the writing of this book. My loving parents provided me with weekly news clippings about New York City schools, thereby helping me to keep this historical work close to the present. As we can see in today's urban schools and in conversations with today's city teachers, almost every tale of confusing and frustrating working conditions told in these pages has a contemporary parallel. My parents' perception of the bitter irony of this historical continuum has been a personal and professional inspiration to me. It is to their faith that progressive workers can create a better world that I dedicate this book.

City Teachers

Introduction

THIS BOOK IS ABOUT teachers' experiences at work in an American city in a period of intense school reform. It is a chronicle of urban teachers' work under intensifying demands, worsening working conditions, and contradictory expectations. It is a story of miscommunication, misunderstandings, and disorder in a city school system, but it is also teachers' story of adaptation and survival in that system. This book is about what it means to be a teacher in modern city schools.

No decade in American history was more noted for its school reform initiatives than the 1920s, and no city seemed to be more exemplary of reform success than New York. From their offices in universities, government agencies, and boards of education, school reformers of the 1920s proposed massive changes in the structure, organization, and purpose of public education. They promised to make schooling the central axis of young people's lives by offering a broad and enlivened curriculum and the most modern facilities. They promoted the professionalization of teaching and liberalized employment laws to open up the occupation to a diverse group of talented young people. Reformers also revised administrative regulations and managerial processes in order to make the local school as efficiently run as a local business, and just as accountable to the public. Politicians and government officials, social reformers, and the popular press heralded the New York City schools of the 1920s as bright intellectual and social machines that scientifically organized and monitored the work of teachers and students. Here was the epitome of modern scientific rationality and order, financial efficiency, and democratic opportunity. On the eve of the 1929 stock market crash, the New York City school system seemed to be one of the great success stories of the nation.

But according to teachers, the schools in which they worked were far from the cleanly rationalized machine that reformers hailed. In the years when New York educators built the largest and most modern school system in the nation, city teachers described dysfunctional working conditions. They described schools as unsystematic workplaces where teachers were regularly challenged with inadequate supplies and facilities, excessive responsibilities, inconsistent and poorly coordinated school policies, and little guidance in accomplishing their daily obligations. Early in their careers teachers found themselves stranded in the middle of a complicated, often nonsensical working environment and facing large classrooms of students who demanded more than any single teacher could ever give. In an era marked by great school reforms, teachers commonly referred to the failure of school reform, to policies that were promised but not implemented, to practices that were not followed and facilities that were not built. Where reformers bore witness to order and progress, teachers saw increasing disorder.

Why was there such a discrepancy between what reformers described and what teachers experienced? That school reformers were so oblivious to teachers' problems in schools is surprising because teachers talked constantly about their working conditions. City teachers in the 1920s tried desperately to explain their experiences to the world outside of the school building, reporting to educators, journalists, and their own associations and unions. On a day-to-day level in the school classrooms, hallways, lunchrooms, and yards, New York City teachers talked with each other about their problems and about their visions of how to create better-functioning schools. But they talked into an echoing silence, the validity of their perspective ignored by those who controlled their working conditions. Teachers' experiences at work in one city in a single decade tell a larger story of the great divide between administrators' ideas and teachers' actual needs and practices.

In this book I argue that city teachers experienced school reform initiatives as confusing and contradictory intrusions into their already stressful workday and that they responded to their chaotic workplace by alternately accommodating, adapting, and resisting certain aspects of their working conditions. Their resistance rarely came through formal political organizations, but rather in day-to-day practices and traditions that furthered their vision of work well done. These traditions of teacher control made up the fabric of their daily work culture: a subtle but pervasive web of knowledge that provided them with familiar guidelines and resources in a chaotic situation. City teachers' understanding of and responses to their working conditions in a period of school reform are the heart of this book.

The decade of the 1920s was certainly not the first time that teachers faced organizational change in their work, but the school reform initiatives of this period were particularly comprehensive and had a notably modern tenor that has characterized urban education ever since. Many of the organizational structures, curricula, and facilities that are familiar to us today were forged in the years after World War I, and the character of modern teachers' work was shaped by the cementing of these same organizational changes. In the first decade of the twentieth century, most American city schools were consolidated into centralized administrative systems with powerful superintendents. By the 1920s, educators were already familiar with the persistent problems of urban schooling , including the financial inequities and administrative snags of a large urban bureaucracy, the complications of managing a large staff, and the sorrows and troubles of many urban students. What distinguished the 1920s was educators' intensified faith that a standard organizational system could solve all these problems. Central to school reformers' visions of the period was the notion that bureaucracy could efficiently deliver a wide range of services through a tightly organized hierarchy of administrators, much like that seen in the highly touted American industries of the period. Scientific rationality and technology would save the modern school. But teachers experienced otherwise.

This book is organized around four recurring themes that characterized teachers' stories of their work in the 1920s. These themes were repeatedly highlighted by teachers as the basic organizational characteristics of city schools, and they serve as a kind of roadmap to the internal ordering of their labor. These themes, and not the visions of school reformers, provide the internalized narrative of city teachers' experiences at work.

The first theme that characterized city teachers' work in this period is that the modern era had seen a steady increase of demands on teachers' time and energy without concomitant support. New York City educators after World War I identified the local school as the central agency that could socialize urban youth away from the demons of modern culture. Increasingly, schools took on the mantel of a social service agency for a diversifying urban student population. The poor, illiterate, unhealthy, or badly behaved child, the young gang member, and the foreign-language-speaking immigrant child were pulled into schools, and the classroom teacher was expected to address all their problems in addition to heightened academic and disciplinary expectations. A broad and unwieldy curriculum demanded that teachers do much more than simply teach class. This intensification of teachers' workload came with no commensurate increase in their control over their resources or time, and no auxiliary support, institutional guidance, or compensation.

The second recurring theme that teachers identified is that they worked in a strangely lonely environment, isolated from their colleagues even as they worked in a crowd of children. Teachers were separated from one another by internal occupational distinctions that physically divided them by building, floor, and classroom, and by hectic schedules that offered no common time. They were also alienated from one another by a popular ideology of professionalism that emphasized teachers' individual responsibility for their work. The professional teacher was defined by educators as a self-restrained and self-monitoring individual, uninterested in financial rewards and oblivious to working conditions. This ideology had powerful implications for teachers' work, furthering their isolation from one another and undercutting attempts to form protective associations or unions. In the nation's largest city, with the largest teaching staff and the most distressed working conditions in the nation, teachers were taught to stand apart from one another and to focus on getting their job done, regardless of the state of their working conditions.

The third theme that emerges is the persistent discrepancy between administrators' and teachers' version of order. Teachers' work was a complicated labor process, built on layers of historical practice and deeply embedded in the social relations, physical working conditions, and personal dynamics of the local workplace. City schools were messy, active places where the uncontrolled sounds, behaviors, and demands of children inevitably ruled the day. City teachers did not only teach students in classrooms, they also worked under a hierarchy of administrative staff, completed endless amounts of bureaucratic paperwork, monitored children in hallways and recess yards, graded papers, supervised tests, and negotiated the daily social relations of a building filled with children and adults. But as teachers continually pointed out, school reform initiatives of the 1920s were often ignorant of the daily human dramas that made up the schoolday. There was a great divide between administrative ideas of a functioning school and teachers' actual needs and practices.

The fourth theme that weaves throughout this book is that teachers responded to their working conditions by alternately accommodating to, adapting to, and resisting certain aspects of their work, surreptitiously claiming some control over their job. This is a story of resistance not by individual teacher activists or organizations but by those regular classroom teachers—the new recruit beginning a 40-year career in the classroom, or the long-term tenured teacher—who learned how to make do in order to accomplish the daily tasks required.

City teachers developed a variety of occupational ethics, informal work traditions, values, and customary practices through which they maintained some individual control over and personal integrity in their job. These traditional practices created a semi-independent working world, or work culture, of teacher knowledge and practice that provided consistency and continuity to an otherwise confusing work situation. By drawing on a fluid collection of informal coping strategies, shortcuts, or tricks of the trade, teachers were able to adapt formal job requirements to the exigencies of the schoolday and, in so doing, exert their own authority at work. Teachers thus developed an odd characteristic of collective isolation, drawing on their colleagues' experiences as resources in order to protect their own spheres of influence in the classroom or the school. Teachers learned the informal rules and practices of teaching on the job, from their colleagues who taught them the ins-and-outs of the work. In this way, new teachers adapted themselves to the organizational structure of the workplace and were themselves changed in the process.[1] As an observer of teachers in the 1930s noted, early in their careers teachers not only learned how to teach, but they also learned how to be "formed by teaching." The experience of teaching literally "makes the teacher."[2]

The adaptive characteristics of work culture went against teachers' interests in the long run, since those strategies that temporarily improved working conditions could discourage organizing for more effective change through teacher unions. Teachers who organized their colleagues to share yard duty, exchange teaching tips, or buffer a particularly harsh administrator accommodated to the structure of the very system that dominated them. By fiddling with the system at the local level, teachers stopped short of openly challenging managerial authority and instigating long-term change. This was the irony of teachers' work culture: While allowing some measure of control, it also undermined the possibility of organizing for real change in the workplace. And while providing an underground collective culture, it furthered teachers' occupational identity as lone individuals. Teachers' underground work culture, then, actually reinforced the stability of the system.

These four themes—the intensification of city teachers' work, the divisions and isolations within the occupation, the divergent meaning of order between teachers and administrators, and teachers' day-to-day adaptive work culture—were the main tendons of teachers' working conditions in city schools. These were the intersecting patterns and practices that shaped both city teachers' work and their responses to that work in modern schools.

THE HISTORICAL SILENCE ON TEACHERS' WORK

My motivation for writing this book originated in my dissatisfaction with the way in which the history of teachers has been written or, more often than not, left unwritten. One reason that teaching has been historically misunderstood is that it is an occupation that defies categorization. Teaching is traditionally women's work, but of all feminized occupations, teaching employs the largest proportion of men. The postsecondary education required to become a teacher narrows most of its personnel to the middle class, yet teaching has traditionally been an avenue for upwardly mobile working class people and ethnic and racial minorities. Notoriously underpaid, teachers have nevertheless earned more than most working-class people, so that the social status of teaching is unclear. Prestigious in stature, much of teachers' work is tedious clerical work, and the physical working conditions of schools can be as gritty and unglamorous as a factory. And even though teachers are well-educated professionals, their work has constantly been the object of school reform initiatives that attempt to closely control their labor.

Historians have also misunderstood and underestimated the complexity of teachers' labor. Labor historians have all but ignored teaching because it has traditionally been understood to be white-collar professional work that did not speak to issues of the working class, even though teaching has been one of the major avenues of working-class mobility throughout the nineteenth and twentieth centuries. Scholars of the professions have also overlooked teaching because of its marginal professional status as a low-paying, feminized occupation, even though teaching became increasingly shaped along a professional model throughout the early twentieth century. Ironically, the very feminized status of teaching has also led feminist scholars to ignore teachers, choosing instead to focus on "groundbreaking" occupations such as law, social work, and higher education, all of which employed far fewer women, and women who were far more privileged, than elementary and secondary school teaching. Historical studies of women's experiences as teachers is curiously slim considering the fact that teaching was one of the top five occupations for women after 1870 and the second-leading occupation for women during the 1920s.[3]

Within educational history, the nature of teachers' work has been examined only within three narrow contexts: the study of classroom pedagogy, school administration and reform, and the development of teachers' political organizations. Histories of classroom practice have shown that teachers have tended to resist progressive educators' efforts to introduce student-centered learning and other creative pedagogy. Such histories offer valuable glimpses into classrooms of the past, but they are limited precisely because they stay inside the classroom, rarely examining the larger context of the schools in which teachers worked or the social and political dynamics that might have limited their ability to promote change.[4] We see the teacher behind the desk, but we do not observe the pressures of the job that the teacher carried with her to that desk.

Another approach to the history of teaching argues that structural changes in school administration in the late nineteenth and early twentieth centuries forced teachers into narrowly defined roles. Like factory workers on assembly lines, teachers are said to have been deskilled, "proletarianized," and dehumanized, losing their workplace autonomy to bureaucratic control mechanisms. That the teaching force was predominately female and the newly empowered school administrators were primarily male has been used to further the argument that the administrative imposition of policy was passively accepted by a feminized teaching force. But here, too, the emphasis on managerial policy and prescriptive curricula eludes the topic of teachers' experience and the extent to which these school policies actually were implemented.[5]

Other scholars have looked to the history of teacher unions for the representation of teachers' voice and experience. Historical accounts of the emergence in the early twentieth century of such teacher unions as the powerful Chicago Teachers Federation, the New York City Teachers Union, and the American Federation of Teachers present a long-ignored history of teacher activism in school, municipal, and national politics. But until the 1960s the bulk of American teachers rarely joined or actively took part in such groups, in part because of often harsh administrative sanctions against union membership, but also because of teachers' own dissatisfaction with union policy and their own reticence or inability to take on union responsibilities. Historical interpretations of teachers through the lens of workers' unions or professional organizations thus render a somewhat narrow vision of the occupation of teaching. Indeed, the reasons that so many teachers did *not* organize hold more clues to understanding teachers' working experience than the exceptional stories of those who did.[6]

Missing from such histories are accounts from the inside of schools that would document the meaning that teachers' work held for them on their own terms. Teachers' experiences of their work were not rooted solely in issues of gender or professionalism or administration or classroom teaching or unions. They were related to all these issues, and the way in which these issues intersected in their daily work processes and conditions. By not attending to teachers' accounts of their experiences, historians have misread the actual conditions of their work.

A NOTE ON METHOD

This book presents a composite picture of teachers' work in New York City schools throughout the 1920s, based on teachers' own accounts and supplemented by other observations of those close to them. The variations, inconsistencies, and contradictions in the portrait attest to the great diversity of working experiences in over 600 New York City schools. Given such diversity, my object has not been to recount meticulous job descriptions at specific moments, but rather to identify the significant issues that the occupation of teaching raised to its workers on a daily basis. This account relies on teachers' descriptions of the daily rhythms of their workday, and the particular stresses and strains that they experienced at work. The focus is on the "commonplaces of schooling": daily occurrences in schools that, when seen through the perspective of different participants, make up the experience of the schoolday.[7] By presenting the world in which teachers worked by drawing on their own descriptions, the book presents broad impressionistic sweeps of recurring themes.

The isolated character of teachers' work has made it difficult for historians to find evidence of their experience. The pace and energy required of teaching has meant that teachers have historically left little trace of their regular interactions, immediate problems, and daily crises at school. Hectic schedules, the frenetic and exhausting task of managing children, and the primacy of each teacher's individual classroom left this highly literate group little time to reflect on or document their work. This makes for a haunting silence in teachers' historical record, a silence all the more ironic because the nature of teachers' work is so noisy and active. Looking to uncover these silences in schools means paying special attention to fragments and shadows of evidence, to recurring echoes of meaning and thinly connected patterns. An ethnography of the everyday world of the workplace 70 years ago has to rely on a variety of sources and conjectures, often looking sideways into the picture presented to us in order to identify teachers' motivations, feelings, and reactions.

To identify the major themes of teachers' work, I began my study with oral histories of those who had taught in New York City schools in the 1920s.[8] In the homes of over a dozen retired teachers, I listened to stories about what it was like to be a teacher in city schools more than 70 years before. I asked not for precise events, but for recurring themes and for the meaning that teaching held for them, for both the average problems and joys, and the exceptional moments of the job. After 30 or 40 years of employment in the school, it was remarkable that these interviewees could isolate only a few years of their career, perhaps because the 1920s were their most formative years at work, when they learned not only how to teach but how to become a teacher. Notable, too, was their generosity and eagerness to talk with a stranger about their work. Many of these teachers thanked me for coming, often remarking that in all their years at work in city schools, nobody had asked them what it was really like to be a teacher. This poignant comment, in and of itself, drove my writing of this book.

The conversations with retired teachers raised my original question about the effect of school reform initiatives on teachers' work and introduced the four themes of intensification of labor, divisions between teachers, the different meanings of order, and teachers' adaptive work culture. I supplemented and corroborated these themes with narrative accounts of teachers' work in contemporary newspapers, administrative papers of the board of education, surveys, research studies, and the papers of special-interest groups, teachers' unions, and associations. One asset for studying teachers in the 1920s is what progressive educator Harold Rugg bitterly criticized as educators' belief in "salvation through statistics" in the period.[9] The 1920s are a gold mine for detailed examinations of schools conducted by graduate students in newly thriving colleges of education and by researchers at the newly financed research bureaus of city school boards. These studies provide glimpses into the daily organization and events in schools, contributing to the descriptive weave of teachers' working conditions on a daily basis. Finally, I drew on sources from city teachers outside of New York—especially Chicago, where working conditions were analogous and where the Chicago Teachers' Federation preserved a wealth of primary documentation on teachers' work. These provided further support for the recurring themes and suggested that the conditions of urban teachers' work were both particular to individual schools *and* universal to all cities.

A few years before this story takes place in New York, the superintendent of schools in another great American city talked about the goals of enlightened school administration. According to Ella Flagg Young, who led the Chicago schools in unprecedented unity with its teachers between 1909 and 1915, it was "isolation in schools" that caused the worst educational problems. City schools in particular were plagued by miscommunication between the different parts of the school organization, a discrepancy in goals and objectives, and a lack of democracy in the daily management of schools. To reform schools, administrators needed to encourage teachers to participate in the running of the school in meaningful ways so that they could articulate their own needs and creative interests as workers. Only then could working conditions in schools be such that teachers could be "awake" and "free" enough to be able to "delight in awakening the spirits of children." Only when the school itself was a truly democratic organization could the school become the "great instrument for democracy."[10] Only by listening to teachers, she implied, could the school truly begin to change.

❦ 1 ❧

Disunity and Dissolution:
The Politics of Teaching Before
World War I

THE NATURE OF URBAN teachers' work in the 1920s was shaped by over
three decades of educational reform that radically changed the working context of urban schools. In the late 1890s, the management of New York City
schools was restructured and transferred from locally based school districts
to a large central superintendency. The centralization of schools severed the
connection between teachers and their communities and, in so doing, created a unified labor group with potential political clout in the city. In the
three decades before World War I, teachers associations and unions in New
York City were active participants in the reformed school system, organizing
for salary improvements, equitable rights for women teachers, and improvements in school management, financing, and curricula. But by the 1920s,
the educational political landscape had changed. New York City teachers
looked remarkably apathetic, their union had deteriorated in both size and
influence, and their surviving representative groups were weak and divisive.
The massive centralized bureaucracy alienated teachers from their communities and, more significantly, from one another. They were silenced by laws
that specified teacher loyalty to the American government, and they were
self-consciously timid under public pressure that they behave "profession-
ally." Divided amongst themselves, New York City teachers in the 1920s
were a politically dispirited group.

How did teachers in the largest school system in America lose the opportunity to become active contributors to their working environment?
What were the conditions that caused teachers in the 1920s to be politically
disconnected from one another and from the waves of school reform initiatives that came upon them? Teachers' political progress and regress between
1890 and 1920 parallel those of other workers in the United States. The
decade prior to World War I was notable for the unprecedented political

activism of American working-class and labor movements. In 1912, the American Socialist party, barely 10 years old, garnered almost 1 million votes for its candidate for president, Eugene V. Debs. In every year between 1916 and 1920, more than 1 million workers went out on strike—a higher proportion of the work force than during any equivalent period before or since. During World War I, labor activism intensified because of labor shortages, consumer inflation, and a booming wartime economy that gave workers improved bargaining positions. In 1919 alone, 4 million workers—one-fifth of the nation's work force— went out on strike. But to many business and government leaders, the country seemed to be under siege from enemies within.

Facing this series of crises through the decade of the teens, President Woodrow Wilson initiated an "alliance" with labor, offering federal protection and mediation between workers and management, including child labor laws, support for organized labor, and hour and wage laws. Akin to Wilson's labor reforms was private business's adoption of worker benefits and corporate welfarism to appease labor. In 1914 Henry Ford announced that in his factories, which produced the popular Model T car, the workday would be reduced from nine to eight hours and the wage increased to $5 a day, double the prevailing wage in neighboring Detroit plants. Other industries soon learned Ford's lesson that higher pay and other benefits would effectively squelch labor activism.

But a much harsher response was dealt to political dissenters. In the heat of the Great War, the federal government instigated a series of policies to suppress political radicalism, including the 1917 Espionage Act under which former presidential candidate Eugene V. Debs was arrested for delivering an antiwar speech and sentenced to 10 years in prison. In 1919, Attorney General A. Mitchell Palmer initiated the notorious Red Scare, arresting thousands of political activists and alleged communists. In December 1919, New Yorkers watched a boat with more than 200 of these radicals, including the well-known anarchist Emma Goldman, sail out of New York harbor under armed guard, their citizenship revoked by the U.S. government. In May 1920, two Italian-born anarchists, Nicola Sacco and Bartolomeo Vanzetti were arrested and charged with murder during the course of an armed robbery. The two men protested their innocence and claimed they were being persecuted for their political beliefs. Millions agreed, protesting their eventual execution in August 1927, but their original arrest and trial marked the dark tenor of the times for American leftists. With the radical front silenced, labor unions underwent a precipitous decline in the 1920s, from over 5 million members in 1920 to 3½ million in 1923.[1]

The story of teacher activists followed a similar pattern through the teens and 1920s. Indeed, as school reformers sought to make education a "profession" that was superior in both pay and prestige to industrial labor, they paid close attention to the tactics of industrial tycoons for subverting labor activism. Like their fellow managers in private industry, school boards initiated both divisive internal organizational schemes and repressive legislation to draw teachers away from unions and to mold a stable and compliant work force. The corporate model of school administration that was introduced by turn-of-the-century school reformers left teachers stranded in a confusing urban bureaucracy that redefined the professional teacher to be obedient to administrative demands. By the end of World War I, New York City teachers had not only lost control over their own daily work, but they had lost control over their very identity as workers.

STRUGGLING FOR CONTROL: THE CENTRALIZATION OF NEW YORK CITY SCHOOLS

At the dawn of the 1920s, the New York City school system was a relatively new phenomenon. There had been schools in the area since the colonial period, when New York was little more than a muddy port village on the southern tip of the Manhattan island, but these were independently run enterprises unsupported by any compulsory-attendance legislation or common system of management. The mid-nineteenth-century common school movement, spearheaded by reformers such as Horace Mann and Henry Barnard, was a nationwide campaign to make common elementary schooling accessible to all children based on the peculiarly American theory that the public had a responsibility to pay for the common equal education of all children, regardless of background. Theory rarely translated to practice for African American children, who in the southern states were denied all schooling and in the North were relegated to segregated schools. For working-class and immigrant children of the nineteenth century, too, schooling was merely a theoretical concept, since it was neither required nor enforced and the labor market gratefully employed children at minuscule wages. But for a vast number of middle-class boys and girls in cities and towns around the country in the 1800s, schooling began to be incorporated into the normal rhythms of childhood.

Until the 1840s, educational provisions in New York City were an eclectic and unregulated collection of local volunteer operations that provided schooling for the diverse communities of the city. Charity schools sponsored by the state's common school fund, private tutoring for the wealthy, segregated schooling for African Americans, church schools for Protestants and Catholics, and a variety of asylums and community schools constituted the types of education that were available to city children. This diversity was hardly a peaceful mix. In a city of increasingly diverse social, religious, and economic interests, local groups battled for students and state finances with such vigor that one historian called them literal "school wars." By mid-century, these wars were muted by compromise as the New York legislature authorized a kind of hybrid public school system for the city whereby 17 local wards ran their own schools, loosely joined at the center by a board of education. Under the ward system, school districts were essentially independent school boards that allowed for distinct differences in hiring policies, financing, and curricula between districts.[2]

The ward system came under a barrage of attack at the turn of the century from a coalition of educators inspired by faith in the power of the state to drive social reform. David Tyack has labeled this group of reformers "administrative progressives" because they believed that effective administrative management could bring about progressive educational and social reform. They argued that through rational scientific planning, schools could be transformed in such a way as to change society and improve the lives of the poor. To that extent, they joined with Jane Addams, Jacob Reis, Booker T. Washington, and other notable progressive reformers of the era who believed that local and individual efforts could "progress" modern society through the terrible inequities of industrial capitalism and into a more egalitarian and truly democratic community. In an increasingly disordered society, these reformers argued, an enlightened corporate model of management could offer the kind of rational controls that would allow economic and social progress.[3]

No public institution in the 1890s seemed more in need of systematic reform than the nation's public schools, and in no place was this more obvious than in New York, a city undergoing rapid demographic, economic, and cultural change. In his widely publicized 1892 survey of contemporary urban schooling, Joseph Meyer Rice identified New York City as typical of American cities in its chaotic management and grim educational environments. The average New York primary school in the 1890s was a "hard, unsympathetic, mechanical drudgery school," with rigid classroom lessons and marked by a "discipline of enforced silence, immobility, and mental passivity." The organization of city schools in the ward system was archaic and inefficient, Rice argued, and it allowed for favoritism and graft in teacher appointments, evaluation, and daily school management. Teachers taught the way that their unenlightened and authoritarian principal demanded of them, so that they actually regressed in their abilities the longer they taught. The New York City school system was a striking example of how a trained teacher "may be reduced to the level of one who has had no training."[4]

The ward system, other critics agreed, was an ineffective means of school financing, and the practice of local patronage made teachers hostage to their employers and subject to corruption. Drawing direct connections between local politics and the image of slumlords and petty graft, reformers connected the ward system and poor schooling with un-American behavior and low morals. Such locally run schools smelled of "saloon politics" charged a Detroit coalition of temperance workers, religious leaders, and municipal politicians. In New York City, critics asserted that local wards were so corrupt that city schools led students on a direct progression from graduation to street life to jail. Everything about New York City schools, asserted Rice, "appears to be involved in a most intricate muddle."[5]

In the 1890s, a small coalition of middle-class business and professional leaders organized to replace the ward system with a centralized city school board structured along a corporate bureaucratic model. Led by Nicholas Murray Butler, president of Teachers College, this group of men administrative progressives was an elite collection of college presidents, bankers, manufacturers, doctors, wealthy philanthropists, and corporate lawyers. Their broad mission was to wrench city schools out of what they believed to be the provincial influence and political graft of city government by abolishing the ward system and replacing it with a small board of education appointed by the mayor and a powerful school superintendent to design, regulate, and monitor reform programs evenly across city neighborhoods. A powerful corporate bureaucracy like this was necessary for efficient and equitable management, argued reformers, just as it was necessary in the complicated state and federal governments or the world's largest manufacturing associations. As New York school executives asserted, "the bigger the problem, the greater the need for centralized responsibility for execution."[6]

New York City teachers disagreed, however, and they organized in defense of the ward system, joining a wide coalition of other opponents, including middle-class community and business leaders, religious leaders, and local political officials. This group argued that the diverse population of the city demanded community schools where class differences, religious preferences, and cultural traditions would be respected. According to teachers and their allies, the centralization of the school system threatened to introduce the worst characteristics of bureaucratic industrialization in which the schools would become a "great perfunctory machine in which the individual parent or teacher is lost."[7]

While teachers shared the concerns of others that a centralized school system would damage community life, they also objected to centralization for specific job-related reasons. The ward system had offered teachers job security, flexibility for negotiation of jobs and rights, local authority within their community boards, and promotions based on classroom experience. Teachers objected to the proposed board of superintendents because it would decrease the authority of the principal with whom teachers had personal contact and, potentially, some room for negotiating professional matters. A board of superintendents would also undercut the traditional senior-ity system of promotion whereby long-tenured teachers moved up into prin-cipalships based on teaching experience and personal references. The reform proposal that teachers would be hired and promoted by objective examina-tions threatened those who had moved up in the system the old way, and it raised the galling prospect of promotions of teachers who performed well on tests but poorly in the classroom.[8]

Teachers' defense of the ward system did not mean that local control had always done them well. New York City teachers in the 1890s held few legal or economic rights, and hardly any identity as independent profession-als. There was no common teacher training school or certification program, no citywide employment policy or salary scale, no central hiring or evalua-tion board. Since teachers' job security was based on patronage with local ward bosses, they remained for the most part an unenlightened and immo-bile group, entrenched in provincial practices and beholden to their patron. Locally controlled schools could and often did mean the continuance of lo-cal discriminations against teachers from ethnic or racial minorities and the persistence of traditional policies such as the exclusion of married women teachers from employment.

Still, according to many teachers, centralization would offer not a better alternative but all of the same problems under the less accountable adminis-trative structure of superintendents. At their most positive, teachers felt am-bivalent about centralization: The reform promised some significant im-provements in working conditions, but it also threatened to take away the benefits of community control over the workplace. Furthermore, a huge bu-reaucracy guaranteed not efficient leadership but rather overly complicated lines of authority that could discourage the cooperative participation of teachers, principals, and the local community in school affairs. In the end, centralization gave teachers the worst of both worlds: a distant and bureau-cratic structure and the loss of local traditions and protections.

Central to the dispute between teachers and managers over the issue of centralization were two different definitions of the concept of efficiency. Where administrative progressives saw centralization bringing a cleanly or-dered system to school management, teachers saw the creation of an ineffi-cient behemoth that threatened to undercut the personal networks and com-munity connections on which their work was based. Teachers persistently argued that the kind of efficiency promoted by school administrators would complicate rather than systematize schools. As one New York City teacher asserted, education was not a process that could be measured like some "standardizable manufacturing process" in the factory or department store. And a federation of teachers associations objected to the authorization of a small administration by explaining: "We do not want a board small enough to get around a table: we want a board big enough to get around the city." Demanding practical, on-site problem solving, teachers argued for a leadership that was familiar with the problems of the schools and knowledgeable enough to devise specific solutions. To teachers, efficiency was not "simplicity of organization" but a broadly representative organization capable of addressing the diverse needs of the city and its "many complicated moral, social, religious, ethical and civic considerations." As the Teachers Union argued in the lead story in its newsletter in March 1916:

> If Efficiency means the demoralization of the school system;
> If Efficiency means dollars saved and human material squandered;
> If Efficiency means discontent, drudgery, and disillusion—
> We'll have none of it!
>
> If Efficiency denotes low finance, bickering, and neglect;
> If Efficiency denotes exploitation, suspicion, and inhumanity;
> If Efficiency denotes larger classes, smaller pay, and diminished joy—
> We'll have none of it!
>
> We espouse and exalt human efficiency—efficiency that spells felicity, loyalty, participation, and right conduct. Give us honorable efficiency and we shall rally to the civic cause.[9]

A notorious example of how administrative notions of efficient management contrasted with teachers' was the ill-fated attempt to institute the platoon school program of Gary, Indiana, to New York City schools in 1914. What became dubbed the Gary Plan was originally designed as a progressive program for elementary schools. Initiated by Gary school superintendent William Wirt in 1907, the proposed plan was that the community school provide a wealth of resources for the child through a unified curriculum of manual and industrial training, academic subjects, and artistic, physical, and moral topics. According to the plan, students would be divided into two "platoons," or groups, which would simultaneously circulate around the school building, using all the facilities in the school. One platoon would take advantage of the gymnasium, auditorium, playground, and shop, while the other platoon focused on academic work in the classroom. Effectively, then, the school building doubled its capacity while students enjoyed a variety of learning experiences. By 1915 "platooning" was a national craze across a wide spectrum of school reformers because it appeared to marry progressive educational practices with economic efficiency. New York City officials were sufficiently impressed by this argument, and Mayor John Mitchel took on the adoption of the Gary Plan to New York schools as a major reform initiative.[10]

But what some administrative-progressives saw as efficiency and progress, others saw as mechanization and penny-pinching. Between 1914 and 1917, New York City teacher groups and community activists vehemently fought the plan, arguing that the platoon system regimented teachers' work and emphasized cost accounting over educational objectives. The newly founded Teachers Union argued that the effect of the Gary Plan was to "get cheaper teachers, specialists who do nothing but keep school, increase the number of hours per day, cut down rest and study time, and increase the size of the classes." Others agreed with even more vehemence: In the autumn of 1917, 10,000 parents and children rioted in various New York neighborhoods to protest the Gary Plan. By the time Mitchel lost his bid at reelection in 1918, the Gary Plan concept had been defeated. However, administrative notions of organizing teaching and schooling around financial accountability and efficiency had only begun. Indeed, the 1920s marked the high point of what one educational historian has described as the tragic "cult of efficiency," with finances, not education, coming to dominate school administrative decisions.[11]

THE RISE AND FALL OF TEACHER ACTIVISM

The centralization of city schools and the emphasis on administrator-defined efficiency was not received passively by teachers. In fact, the impersonality of the new centralized system allowed teachers to develop a new sense of occupational identity as workers with newly developed political responses. When teachers were no longer beholden to local officials in the ward system, they were free to organize for their democratic rights within the larger institutional structure. With the centralization of city schools in the 1890s came a period of unprecedented political activity among American teachers, who organized to fight for salary raises, job protections, and employment benefits. In the first two decades of the twentieth century, teachers in Chicago, Atlanta, Buffalo, Pittsburgh, Detroit, and other urban centers organized militant campaigns for recognition as political players in the shaping of school policy and their own working conditions. Between 1919 and 1920 alone, more than 143 local teacher unions were organized.[12]

The greatest figurehead of American teacher activism in the teens was the Chicago Teachers Federation. Founded in 1897, the Federation was notorious for both its size and its political prestige through World War I. At the height of its influence, more than half of all Chicago elementary school teachers were members of the Federation. Under the leadership of the dynamic Margaret Haley, the Federation affiliated with the Chicago Federation of Labor in 1902, and in 1916 it became Local 1 of the newly formed American Federation of Teachers. In a series of highly publicized actions, the Federation successfully challenged corporate tax deductions that undercut teachers' salaries and closely monitored employment policies for teachers. Haley specifically opposed the new corporate model of management in school administration, labeling the priority on economic efficiency as nothing less than the "factoryization" of education under which the teacher would become "an automaton, a mere factory hand, whose duty it is to carry out mechanically and unquestioningly the ideas and orders of those clothed with the authority of position, and who may or may not know the needs of the children or how to minister to them." In her notorious 1904 speech before the National Education Association (NEA), "Why Teachers Should Organize," Haley laid out her own reform proposals not only for the organization of protective unions for teachers, but also for an expanded notion of teacher professionalism that would counter the depersonalizing effects of business management theory applied to schools. In her vision of the truly reformed school, teachers would have the opportunity to develop progressive pedagogy, improve educational practice, and participate democratically in school management.[13]

New York City teachers were also active in city and occupational politics in the first two decades of the twentieth century. Women teachers took up several campaigns to assert their rights as workers and to abolish gender inequities in the occupation. New York City women teachers fought for equal salary schedules with men beginning in 1900. Over 14,000 teachers joined the Interborough Association of Women Teachers and successfully abolished the separate salary scales for men and women teachers and principals in 1911. Women teachers also organized against a law that prohibited married women teachers from employment in the school system. Marriage laws, which were common in small school districts across the country through the 1940s, were based on the argument that married women should be at home caring for their families and that they did not need to work because their husbands supported them. But in fact many married women *were* interested in teaching to such an extent that a great number of cities and towns across the nation passed legislation in order to prohibit it. New York City's ban was imposed by the board of education in 1903, but women teachers immediately joined with other feminists to challenge the law in 1904, making New York City one of the few school districts in the country that allowed married women to teach. New York City activists next took on a 1911 regulation that prohibited mothers from employment in the system, and three years later they succeeded in making New York only the fourth American city to grant women teachers leaves of absence for childbirth.[14]

Male and female radical teachers also joined to organize what became the New York City Teachers Union in 1913 in an attempt to promote democratic policies in the board of education. Supported by such progressive luminaries as the educator John Dewey and the feminist writer Charlotte Perkins Gilman, the Teachers Union was a visionary organization that promoted teacher participation in the design and implementation of board of education policies, teachers' freedom of speech, the expansion of democratic school management, and improved working conditions and salaries. The Union was a highly visible institution, organized as Local 5 of the newly formed American Federation of Teachers, affiliated with the American Federation of Labor in 1916, and supported by many of the city's intellectual elite and leftist activities. Indeed, to many teachers, it was known more for its radical political agenda, which went beyond the improvement of teachers' working concerns toward broader social reform issues. This breadth of interest and radical platform eventually contributed to the repression and demise of the Union.

For all the accomplishments and notoriety of these radical groups, most New York City teachers were not political activists. Teachers who were involved in occupationally related organizations were far more likely to work within their local professional associations. From the turn of the century through the 1920s, up to 70 independent teacher associations existed in New York City. Local borough associations enrolled up to half of all eligible teachers, and many teachers were also members of subject or grade-level associations, for example, special associations for teachers of kindergarten or high school, teachers of special subject areas, and Jewish and Catholic teachers. Teacher associations were not radical political organizations but self-interested protective groups that held mainstream views about the role of schools and teachers. Local associations provided professional supports for teachers, sponsoring lectures, demonstration lessons, and coursework. The Brooklyn Teachers' Association, the largest local association in the nation, organized a cooperative buying group that arranged trade discounts for participating members, and Brooklyn businesses provided interest-free loans and special services for members. The associations also offered social activities that were geared primarily for teachers, including special concerts, parties, lecture series, and vacation tours for school holidays. Associations' political activities centered on issues of immediate concern to teachers, including lobbying the state legislature for increased salaries and benefits, and negotiations with the board of education over evaluation and rating procedures. Teacher association members were a notoriously conservative group, relying on their leaders to lobby for benefits and overwhelmingly opposing any affiliation with organized labor or politically left-wing parties or causes. For the most part, associations served as a combination of social network, educational agency, and professional advocate without challenging the structure of city school leadership.[15]

The lack of political motivation on the part of many association members clearly frustrated even those leaders who might have opposed a more militant organization such as the Union. In 1914, for example, the chairman of the school problems committee of the Brooklyn Teachers' Association proposed the creation of a bureau of research to gather statistics on teachers' working hours that would support their argument for salary increases. Members rejected the proposal, expressing concern about the cost of such a venture. But as the chairman reflected bitterly, members showed no such parsimony about funding social events, since in the same report, a jubilant chairman of the committee on the swimming pool announced that teachers had pledged $4,000 toward the construction of an Association pool.[16]

Teacher associations' preoccupation with the concerns of their own interest group also led them to act divisively against other teachers, a fact that contributed to the subsequent failure of collective teachers' activism in the city. When women teachers fought for equal-pay laws, they were opposed by more than 600 men teachers and principals, who formed an Association of Men Teachers and Principals of New York. The men countered the women's cause by arguing that women did not deserve equal pay because they were intellectually inferior, they did not require the same standard of living as men, and the policy would lead more women to avoid marriage.[17]

The Teachers Union membership was also narrowed by divisions in the teaching force. To a great extent, Union leaders—who were primarily Jewish male high school teachers—acted as a special-interest group of their own. The Union supported a merit system of promotion, arguing that a neutral system of evaluation would allow more mobility for Jewish and immigrant teachers who were not hooked into the traditional local patronage systems. Ironically, then, the Union agreed with administrators who were intent on decreasing teachers' traditional local authority. The Union also promoted a single salary scale according to which high school teachers were paid significantly more than elementary school teachers, thereby alienating the 85% of the teaching force—primarily women—in the elementary schools. Union membership was further limited by its broad agenda of social and educational reform—issues that did not appeal to teachers' more immediate concerns with their own salary. The effect of these divisions was devastating for the Union: Its membership barely rose above 5% of the New York City teaching force.[18]

The case of the Teachers Union offers insight into the complex and ironic state of teacher politics in New York in the years before World War I. Teachers had supported the ward system of school governance because it meant personal connections and occupational security. But this worked only for those teachers who *had* personal connections, working against "outsiders" to the system, including Jewish teachers and married women. The centralization of schools replaced the personal connection of job security with allegedly objective measures of evaluation and promotion. This system could potentially help outsiders, but the centralization of school management also furthered special-interest-group politics among teachers, because so many groups across the city were now obliged to lobby one central agency for protection and support. Centralization thus created competition and divisiveness among groups of teachers. As the city administration centralized, teachers divided. By the end of the teens, teachers' representative groups were more isolated and powerless than they had been before centralization. These conditions were only worsened by the politics of the home front during the Great War.

POLITICAL REPRESSION AND OCCUPATIONAL DIVISION

Teachers' political work, especially their work in the Union, was undercut by more than internal occupational divisions. In the wake of World War I, government forces silenced radicals in the occupation of teaching as quickly as they repressed other political leftists. School administrators in the late teens were noticeably anxious about the growth of teacher associations and unions. The problem was not only one of politics, but also of economics. There was a drastic shortage of teachers as the nation prepared for war and qualified applicants turned to higher-paying wartime work. Simultaneously, public critiques of low teacher salaries, difficult working conditions in schools, and undemocratic practices in school administration drove potential teachers away from the occupation or into the arms of the multiplying teacher unions. Faced with a steep decline in prospective teachers and a sharp increase in school enrollments, school administrators at the dawn of World War I faced a critical teacher shortage, a public that was apparently losing faith in the school system, and an increasingly irritable teacher force.[19]

For good reason, then, did the editorial board of the *American School Board Journal* in September 1919 ask its readers if the nation's schools were facing an impending "breakdown." A looming "teacher crisis" threatened the very order and authority of schools' administrative structure. This was not unlike the crisis caused by the organization of workers in industry in the immediate postwar era, and the administrative response was not unlike that of industrial managers facing the expansive growth of unions. Like Attorney General Palmer's Red Scare attack on radicals in 1919 and 1920, city school officials joined with government agents in an all-out persecution of radical teachers.

In his exhaustive study, *Are American Teachers Free?*, Howard Beale chronicled the repression of teachers, ostensibly for reasons of national security, during and immediately after World War I. Across the country, thousands of teachers were suspended or dismissed or their teaching licenses were revoked for not abiding by school board loyalty regulations. The special restrictions on teachers were justified by the argument that since teachers were in charge of the social and intellectual education of all American youth, they were in a particularly strategic position to undermine national security. Unlike other citizens, argued legislatures, teachers simply could not hold "one set of opinions for the classroom and another for the public platform." [20] Under attack was any teacher who expressed pacifist or antiwar sentiment; refused to take required loyalty oaths, salute the flag, or teach patriotic songs; did not advise students to buy Liberty Bonds; expressed any pro-German sentiment or belonged to any communist or socialist group; or, in at least one case, was married to a German citizen. In New York State, the notoriously repressive Lusk Laws, enacted in 1918 and not repealed until 1923, were designed to ensure a narrow version of loyalty among New York teachers: They required all schools in the state to teach courses in citizenship and patriotism, to display an American flag, and to provide a program for saluting the flag. The laws banned from the schools any textbook containing matter that was "seditious" or "disloyal" and provided for the prosecution of any teacher or administrator who permitted such a book in a school. The final and most contentious provision was the requirement for teachers to sign a pledge of loyalty and for the removal of any school employee who uttered or enacted "treasonable or seditious" statements or acts. In New York City at least 17 teachers were dismissed or fired and more than 50 were transferred, rebuked, or denied promotion for refusing to uphold the Lusk Laws. Three DeWitt Clinton High School teachers were suspended for behavior in the classroom that was considered subversive: One teacher was found guilty of allowing a student to write an antiwar letter to President Wilson; a second was guilty of allowing his students to debate the value of the war, Liberty Bonds, anarchism, and the American system of government; the third was accused of preventing patriotic statements in his classroom. A high school Latin teacher in Brooklyn was dismissed because, as a Quaker, she could not support the war effort. A German-born elementary teacher in Brooklyn was dismissed because she refused to state that she hated her native country, and a colleague at the same school was suspended for six months for opposing the draft. [21]

The Teachers Union fiercely opposed the Lusk Laws and was in turn accused of being antipatriotic by more conservative groups. The three fired teachers at DeWitt Clinton were Teachers Union members, and the Union's two leaders, Henry Linville and Abraham Lefkowitz, were both investigated under the Lusk Laws. Other teacher groups attacked the Union, passing resolutions against the organization of teacher unions and the hiring of socialist teachers, and initiating their own investigations against them. The Brooklyn

Teachers Association supported the inquisition of teachers accused of disloyalty, arguing that teachers in the classroom "wield the weapons which can and must foil Bolshevism and anarchy."[22]

The divisions between teachers were perhaps as debilitating to the Union as were the repressive laws. When the huge and legitimate Brooklyn Teachers Association opposed the tiny Teachers Union, it broadcast that there was only one successful model of teacher activism in New York City. By the end of the war, most New York City teachers had learned their lesson that collective activism with a vision as promoted by the Teachers Union was not a viable model of political action. As historian Wayne Urban argues, the story of the New York City Teachers Union is a story of ideological battles of the intellectual left more than it is a story shared by most teachers.[23] Further alienating the Union from the perspective of most teachers were school administrators' tactics in developing and enforcing alternative models for teachers' political action that molded teachers into a more pliable and submissive force.

CONTROL THROUGH DEMOCRACY

In the years just prior to the 1920s, American teachers' very identity as workers was reshaped by an administrative-led reform movement known as democracy in education. The democracy in education movement drew directly from contemporary labor management theories of "industrial democracy" that were conceived by industrial capitalists as a mechanism for promoting cooperation between managers and workers. Central to this emerging philosophy of industrial relations was the notion that labor and management were mutually supporting allies, joined in a common project of efficient production. By means of welfare programs such as company unions, shop committees, and employee representation plans, the worker was supposed to be lifted from the position of mechanical drone to one of a "proprietor" who shared interests with management, and the ideal workplace would become, as historian Daniel Rogers describes it, "a moral organism" and a "community of purpose and endeavor."[24]

Labor activists argued that industrial democracy was only a thinly veiled attempt to secure worker loyalty to management. The image of cooperation and any semblance of reality behind it, unionists pointed out, was controlled by the same management that prohibited worker-based organizations such as unions because they promoted worker interests over capitalist gains. Under corporate welfare plans, workers might be given benefits and accorded the image of equality, but the rules of the land were determined by a superior managerial authority. Management thus controlled the ground rules for both worker production and worker dissent.[25]

School administrators paid close attention to the industrial democracy agenda and adopted it to their own problem of teacher activism. The rhetoric of the democracy in education movement drew directly on nationalist images of American democracy—a particularly powerful image in post–World War I America. Indeed, the lesson of the world war was that democratic ideals, respect for diversity, and cooperation were far more effective than dictatorship. School reformers urged administrators to make their schools little democracies based on collegial values rather than autocracies organized simply for "narrow, technical efficiency." The image of the benevolent and democratic school administrator was also contrasted with the unionist teacher who was characterized as particularly *un*democratic. Advocates of democracy in education argued that the solution to these supposedly tyrannical unionists was not "antagonism and repression" by administrators but the removal of conditions that led to the problem: "The cure for the ills of democratic school government"—meaning unionization—"is more democracy." According to school administrators, the truly "professional" teacher was one who accommodated to and voluntarily participated in the expectations of the established authority structure. The professional teacher was thus an obedient teacher and a better worker who was "more competent in instruction, more responsive to leadership, and more loyal to schools."[26]

Furthering the construction of the new professional teacher as a loyal participant in democracy, school administrators promoted such notions as teamwork, partnership, and cooperation. But such teamwork could only be initiated by administrators, who were to instruct teachers how to be cooperative. Teachers were apparently too long accustomed to being passive workers in an administratively controlled system, and it was now administrators' responsibility to raise teachers to a more professional level by offering more opportunities for contribution to the school. If a teacher was found to be narrow-minded, argued the president of the New York City Board of Education, administrators had only themselves to blame for "keeping her in a system so mechanical as to limit too much the exercise of her initiative and invention." Or, as one principal blatantly phrased his responsibility to encourage cooperation among his teachers: "We should get much more out of teachers than we do."[27]

Administrative rhetoric about teachers' cooperation and loyalty to the schools was institutionalized in teacher councils that were founded in over 80 cities around the nation between 1910 and 1922. The mission of teacher councils was well aligned with that of the administrative democracy in education movement, because teacher representation to school governance was to be controlled by the guiding principle of obedience to administrative authority. Teacher councils were an advisory institution only and were never intended to be an avenue for real grievances or an agency for significant change in teachers' working conditions. Indeed, the New York State commissioner of education specifically warned that the new teacher councils not be used by "disaffected" members of the teaching staff "who suffer under the delusion of being oppressed." Such teachers raise enough "misunderstanding and antagonism" that they are likely to cause more damage to teacher–administrator relations than even an antagonistic superintendent or principal.[28]

The New York City Teachers' Council was founded in 1913 with a mission to act as an advisory council to the board of education, and from the beginning it represented the controlled version of democracy. Its membership of 45 teachers was not elected from the teaching force at large, but from representatives of teachers' professional associations. Nor was the group given any authority: The mission of the Council was to research questions submitted by the board of education and to issue recommendations in response. Philosophically and politically, the New York City Teachers' Council mirrored its parent administrative body. In its early years, the Council leadership assured the board of education of its loyalty and professional behavior. According to its president in 1917, the Teachers' Council was an example of the "harmony, efficiency, and whole-souled co-operation" that teachers were capable of, and it disproved any assumptions that teachers could not meet together without causing dissension and disruption in the school system. Furthermore, the Teachers' Council proved how hard teachers could work and *would* work for a greater cause by willingly taking on "new and uncompensated burdens." In addition, the Council stood by the administration in its condemnation of teachers accused of disloyalty to the nation during wartime, and it denounced the Socialist party and conducted surveys of radicalism among New York teachers. According to its own leadership, the Council made no attempt to "infringe upon the rights of the superintendents of school" but merely to offer opinions and support of the central school administration.[29]

Teacher activists also had a vision of a democratically representative Teachers' Council, but it differed widely from that promoted by administrators. The difference between the two versions highlights the extent to which administrative reformers specifically designed their model of teacher councils for the purpose of silencing the voice of activist teachers. Ella Flagg Young, superintendent of Chicago schools in the early twentieth century, was one of the more articulate advocates of a teacher council that would not only provide representative responsibilities for teachers in school management, but would also address the chronic problem that Young defined as "isolation in the schools"—or the lack of coordination and communication between teachers and administrators. Margaret Haley, the president of the Chicago Teachers Federation, took Young's vision of teachers' participation in schools and expanded it, arguing that the very social integrity of the school depended on teachers taking part in the design and management of the curricular and philosophical foundations of the school. Haley argued for a teacher council that would both draw teachers into the integral professional issues of education and that would transform the school organization. Given authority, teachers would evolve from mere pedagogues to skilled social servants, and the role of schools would change from mere centers of instruction to places of social justice. If teachers took on democratic responsibilities in the school, Haley argued, the school would become a democratizing vehicle for society.[30]

The New York City Teachers Union also drew on the notion of democracy in education as a transformative force for teachers and schools. In its early years, the Union called for the organization of self-governing school and district councils, as well as elected teacher representation on the board of education. To Henry Linville, the first president of the Union, the truly democratic school would be a beehive of activity where teachers would take part in identifying the problems of the school and working toward solutions. While arguing for teacher representation in the larger city administration, the Union also emphasized the importance of individual school councils where teachers could address problems in their immediate workplace, including the curriculum, administrative supervision, and physical working conditions. In such councils, teachers could identify the working problems of most immediate concern to them and collectively effect change. Like Young and Haley, Linville believed that the process of democracy was as important as its product and that merely implementing the structures of representative democracy would not in and of itself create a democratic workplace.[31] Representative councils needed real authority to challenge and reform the structures of the modern bureaucratic school.

The New York City Teachers Union recognized the great disparity between its vision of democracy in education and that of school administrators, and, not surprisingly, it fought the Teachers' Council almost from the beginning, noting the restricted format and opportunities of the Council. In particular, the Union objected to the limited representation of the Council whereby teachers were elected from professional associations, thus ignoring those who were unaffiliated with a group. The Union also condemned the Council for its conservative political stands, particularly its criticism of socialist teachers—who were all Union members—and its support of the board of education's persecution of those teachers during the war years.[32]

By the 1920s, the Teachers Union had severed all relationships with the Teachers' Council and referred to the organization with vituperative distaste as an "ineffective, time-serving and reactionary body" and a "public nuisance" that played no useful role in the school system.[33] But by this time, the

Union itself had fallen out of the public eye. Its visionary mission was popular among the city's progressives but far less popular among rank-and-file teachers, particularly after the board of education's public accusations and firings of Union teachers from city schools for antiwar and socialist affiliations during the war.

CONCLUSION

The reorganization of the New York City school system between 1890 and World War I had long-lasting effects on teachers' occupational identity and the ways in which teachers could respond to their working conditions. Under the centralized school system managed by a corporate-style bureaucracy, teachers were disconnected from their traditional local roots and their traditional methods of promotion. The early history of New York City teachers showed a high point of unified political activism when teachers organized for occupational reform and social change. But teachers' political activism was squashed by legal regulations that persecuted and silenced their most radical voices. In a further attempt to shape teacher politics, school administrations promoted an ideology of professionalism that furthered teachers' affiliation with and under administrators.

As much as any political repression or reorganization, the emergence of administrator-defined efficiency as a guiding ideology had the most significant effect on teachers' ability to control their own work. Beginning with the debates over centralization, teachers and administrators articulated opposing views of the "efficient" school. Administrators envisioned a centralized hierarchical power that would create a tightly functioning educational machine. But inside schools, teachers saw an efficient organization as one that was more flexible, adaptable, and locally based. To teachers, an efficient school was one that was capable of addressing the immediate local problems of coordination, communication, and synchronization inherent in a school building. An efficient school, according to teachers, included their voice and authority. But the guiding philosophy of democracy in education became a code for administrative control of teacher activism in schools and, like the broader term of industrial democracy, it became a way for administrators to break the back of teacher organizations and to fold teachers into the bottom of a school organizational hierarchy. Divided by organizational structure, political repression, and professional ideology, teachers were too weak to fight for their vision of an efficient workplace. But as we shall see in the next chapter, teachers were already primed for the failure of any semblance of collective work by changes in the internal organization of teaching personnel.

~ 2 ~

To Be a Teacher: The Shaping of an Occupation

NEW YORK CITY WAS A GREAT place to be a teacher in the 1920s. The New York Board of Education offered the highest salaries in the country, liberal and equitable employment laws, and excellent personnel benefits. The school system was also rapidly expanding, so there were hundreds of new jobs opening every year through most of the decade. A system of free public high schools, colleges, and teacher training institutes prepared prospective teachers, and a competitive certification process guaranteed excellent preparation. Unlike other city school boards, the New York Board of Education had no quotas for African American or Jewish applicants, and women and men were hired and paid equally. By all appearances the New York school system seemed to invite all the diversity and promise of the city itself into its staff.

But official policies of employment equity disguised more deeply ingrained divisions within city schools. Formal employment policies in the system and informal personnel practices in the schools were implicitly prejudiced against teachers from certain cultural, ethnic, and class backgrounds. Men and women teachers faced vastly different messages about their suitability as teachers and were channeled to specific levels of the occupation. The entire teacher education process was one of shaping individuals to conform to a model of professional identity and behavior that was laden with cultural and gendered prejudices. The process of becoming a teacher was not only a process of learning skills for classroom instruction, but also one of learning the defined behaviors and values of a profession. The social world of teacher training schools and employment policies acted as its own sifting and sorting mechanism, narrowing the pool of potential teachers and infusing the occupation with normative assumptions about the personal and cultural qualities of the ideal "professional" teacher. If becoming a teacher meant anything, it meant literally becoming a certain kind of person.

Once new teachers survived the training and employment process and found themselves employed in a school building, their very identity remained under constant public scrutiny. Schools were not just places where students learned and teachers taught; they were also places where people interacted with one another and with the organization of which they were a part. It was the social relations of the school that could make the difference between a positive or negative experience for both students and teachers. As Willard Waller observed in his 1932 study of American teachers, people "who live together in the school, though deeply severed in one sense, nevertheless spin a tangled web of interrelationships; that web and the people in it make up the social world of the school."[1]

This chapter examines how that "tangled web" of social relations in the school affected the way that city teachers experienced and responded to their working conditions. Teachers were, as Waller noted, "deeply severed" from one another as the result of their training and employment policies. In the school building, teachers and principals were allowed to further those divisions by creating an ambiance of exclusion and prejudice that belied any liberal laws. These internal personnel divisions affected the way teachers were able to respond to their work as political actors. To a great extent, the school system mirrored the larger metropolis: Dynamic New York City of the 1920s was both the epitome of modern liberalism and diversity and a caricature of provincialism and local bigotry. United only by their common identity as employees of the New York City school system, teachers were both trained to and allowed to continue internal divisions.

WORKING IN NEW YORK CITY

To Angelo Patri, principal of a Manhattan elementary school, New York City in the 1920s was a spectacular place to live and work. Patri, himself an immigrant from Italy, affectionately described New York in the mid-1920s as

> the biggest, noisiest, liveliest, crudest, dirtiest, most entrancing city in the world. You can find a bit of everything here that was ever produced in the world. You will find beauty and ugliness side by side. You will find cruelty and loving kindness on the same block, but it is all lovely. I like New York best at night; not on the street but up on top of one of the sky-scrapers where I can look out over the City and it lies spread out like a garden of light. There is every color of light imaginable. It lies in spots and splashes and comes in waves and little twinkles, and altogether it is the most dazzling picture one could possibly see out of fairyland. All the noise and confusion and crudity of the city below is wiped out in a deep blue velvety shadow. Then you know how wonderful New York can be. . . . It is all very beautiful and all very awful.[2]

Although it was in many ways unique among American cities, New York was also an icon for all urban life, its symbols of size and speed serving as the epitome of modernism. This image alone drew thousands of immigrants from abroad and from around the nation to New York to experience its economic opportunities and excitements. The expanding urban population created entirely new communities and formed new ethnic residential neighborhoods, causing the Irish novelist Shaw Desmond to describe New York as not a city but "a city of cities." The construction of apartment and office buildings, bridges, and public subway lines led a bewildering pace of physical urban growth, while the increased number of automobiles, movie theaters, and other cultural signals of the 1920s marked frenetic social modernization. New York, wrote a visiting Frenchman in the 1920s, "is a perpetual thunderstorm."[3]

Probably what characterized the city most on first sight was the density and diversity of its population. The city's population grew from 4½ million in 1910 to 7 million in 1930, with an average of half a million immigrants entering the city each year. There was also internal migration from around the nation. A quarter of a million black Americans moved from the South to New York in the 1920s, doubling the black population of the city so that by 1930 they constituted almost 5% of the population. Rural Americans also moved to New York in droves, following a pattern first noted in the 1920 census of more Americans living in cities than in the country. The population of New York in the 1920s was not only large but diverse, a tangle of new immigrant arrivals and old immigrant cultures. New York had one of the largest Jewish populations in the world, huge Italian and Irish communities, and emerging communities of Asians and Middle Easterners. Well over half of the city's population between 1910 and 1930 were second- and third-generation immigrants, and as late as 1930 one-third of the population was foreign-born—in spite of two recent immigration restriction laws.[4]

Residential neighborhoods marked the informal but persistent boundaries between the different classes, ethnicities, and races in the city. As select populations grew, they were drawn or pushed to certain areas of the city to become homogeneous and segregated islands in an ocean of diversity. In the 1920s there were distinct communities of Chinatown and Little Italy on the Lower East Side of Manhattan; Jewish districts in Manhattan, the Bronx, and Brooklyn; havens for the rich on Manhattan's Upper East Side and residential apartments for the middle class on the Upper West Side; and an alternative community of intellectuals, political radicals, and feminists in Greenwich Village.

Most distinctive of all was Harlem in northern Manhattan. During the teens, southern black Americans had begun a migration to northern cities to trade the persistent poverty and political disenfranchisement of the rural

South for work in industry. Most southern blacks came north with few skills, minimal education, and even less money, and when they settled in Harlem, the district turned almost immediately into a densely crowded, poverty-stricken ghetto. Overcrowding pushed up the price of even the most dilapidated apartment; rampant unemployment spurred crime, gambling, juvenile delinquency, prostitution, and chronic health problems. In spite of the misery, Harlem still attracted black Americans, drawn in part by moments of relief offered by the black political organizations and artistic movements of the 1920s. Harlem offered a residential and cultural refuge from white America, a distinct and proud black metropolis characterized by its own "renaissance" of literary, visual, and musical arts. As James Weldon Johnson wrote in 1930, the cultural life of Harlem was "a phenomenon, a miracle straight out of the skies."[5]

For all the residential segregation among races, classes, and cultures, New Yorkers interacted across boundaries in the city's many public spaces, including Central Park and dozens of smaller neighborhood parks, the subways, streets, and squares, and in public institutions such as hospitals, government offices, post offices, and the popular boardwalks and amusement parks of Coney Island. Differences between groups were also assuaged by a booming new consumer culture. In the 1920s, the new film industry changed popular assumptions about proper behavior, and in no place was this social shift more apparent than in New York, where the capacity of its movie theaters increased eight times while the city's population only doubled. Radio sound waves also exploded into the home in the early 1920s, and on the street a vibrant, visual popular culture was available in the theaters of Times Square and the penny arcades around the city. One visitor commented that postwar New York was "a vast cash register [that] toils night and day to amuse—and charges accordingly." The very tenor of the city was one of hurtling speed, carelessness, and consumption like that of "a storming-party hurrying towards an unknown goal."[6]

No public institution was more representative of the growth and diversity of New York in the 1920s than the public school. One million children attended city public schools through most of the 1920s, and an average of 21,000 new students entered the schools every year during the decade, many of these first- and second-generation immigrants. Expanding enrollment led the board of education to create a smorgasbord of educational options for the greater variety of students attending school. Adolescents who were legally required to attend a certain amount of secondary schooling could choose from specialized programs in commercial, technical, and industrial education, night and continuation schools, and standard academic high schools. A few high schools were single-sex, including the prestigious college preparatory all-boys Stuyvesant High School and the all-girls Julia Richman, which specialized in vocational education for the commercial and clerical trades. Younger students attended local elementary and junior high schools, and students with special needs attended classes for the handicapped in "ungraded" classrooms.[7]

Increased enrollment meant that New York schools needed teachers badly. The teaching force grew from 20,000 teachers in 1920 to 33,600 in 1930, with more than a thousand new teaching positions opening every year. At the same time, the years immediately following World War I were marked by a severe teacher shortage both nationally and regionally. Wartime production had spurred a number of high-paying postwar occupations that attracted potential teachers, particularly men returning from the war. The decline of potential candidates, combined with regular retirements from the system, meant that in one year alone there were more than 1,400 job openings in city elementary and secondary schools and barely a thousand qualified applicants.[8]

The demand for teachers forced an improvement in salaries and personnel policies so that by the mid-1920s, the New York City Board of Education offered to its job applicants unusual personnel privileges and abolished most formal and informal restrictions against married women, African Americans, and applicants from outside the local school community or metropolitan area. Three salary raises for New York City teachers were implemented by the state legislature between 1920 and 1926, so that by the middle of the decade the average teacher salary was substantially more than that for blue-collar and lower-level white-collar work for men and women. Even with the persistent inflation of the 1920s, which significantly modified the purchasing power of salary increases, New York City teachers earned more than other city and state employees and above the average income of all American workers.

New York City schools offered teachers a compulsory pension plan, established in 1917 as the first plan in the nation with equal contributions by the school board and teacher. Employment with the board of education also included occupational benefits of internal job mobility, maternity leave and sabbaticals, and a schedule that freed summers for other work or activities. Teaching was a job with a great deal of stability: Most teachers earned and kept their permanent licenses after the three-year probationary period. The average amount of experience for New York teachers in 1927 was 11 years, indicating that teaching was not only a secure job, but one that teachers chose to keep. The job also promised social prestige and the intellectual excitement of working in a cohort of highly educated individuals. In the late 1920s, as many as one-third of all women and two-thirds of all men teachers and administrators in New York City had *more* than four years of higher education in a period when nationally less than 7% of 18- to 24-year-olds even entered college. Compared to many jobs available to women and men just emerging from the working class, teaching was a white-collar job that promised unusual career security and satisfactions. Finally, teaching was an attractive job because it seemed to involve some personal interaction and creativity, in contrast to the typically stultifying work in the modern clerical pool or on the assembly line. Teachers may have loved teaching, but, in fact, the occupation also offered them the kinds of benefits and securities that constituted a lifetime investment.[9]

THE CREATION OF THE PROFESSIONAL TEACHER

But not everybody could become a teacher. To consider a career in the New York City public school system, applicants needed a high school education at the minimum. This requirement in and of itself sharply narrowed the field of prospective candidates because barely a third of American adolescents even attended high school in the early twentieth century, and less than half of those actually graduated. Even in New York City, where high school enrollments increased dramatically during the 1920s, only half of all New York City youth attended secondary school. The first high schools in New York City opened in the 1880s; by 1929 about 100,000 students were enrolled in 38 academic high schools. A lesser number attended the great variety of alternative secondary schools, including vocational and trade schools and evening schools. Most of those enrolled in the academic high schools were from native-born white middle-class families, although some immigrant groups—particularly the children of Eastern European Jews—attended the new high schools at increasing rates.[10]

One reason for low secondary school enrollment rates was the demands of the labor market. Through the 1920s, New Yorkers over the age of 16 had relatively free rein to enter the labor market, and a high school diploma had little value except in white-collar jobs, such as clerical and secretarial work—jobs that remained far beyond the dreams of most working-class youth. In cities like New York where it was relatively easy for a young person to find an unskilled job, and where the cost of living was high, secondary schooling was an option for only those families who could financially afford to invest in education for the future rewards of white-collar wages. For those immigrant and black New Yorkers who did enter high school, their educational achievement was more often a result of prior economic achievement than a cause of it. A similar economic dynamic was at play for young women. New white-collar jobs in secretarial, clerical, medical, and communications fields were the fastest-growing occupations in the postwar era, and they were designed specifically as low-paying, semiskilled work for women

with a high school education. The high school qualification effectively excluded most ethnic and working-class women from the new occupations.
High schools thus played a major role in creating a dual career market for
women, providing white middle-class women with the opportunity to enter
certain occupations while denying such opportunity to others. Secondary
schooling was required for white-collar jobs, but access to secondary schooling was determined by class and ethnicity. Thus high school acted as a kind
of sorting mechanism for white-collar employers, sifting out the poorest and
most marginalized from the applicant pool.[11]

The entrance requirements for teaching also regulated the social background of potential teachers. The qualifications for a teaching certificate in
New York City schools became increasingly difficult to achieve in the 1920s.
For prospective elementary school teachers, the number of years required in
teacher training school doubled during the 1920s, increasing from two years
to three in 1923, and then to four years in 1929. To become a teacher in the
secondary schools required a four-year college degree. In 1929 the board of
education also raised the minimum grade required to pass the state teachers'
examination. The extension of teacher training requirements was part of
American educators' plan to improve the professional status of the occupation to be more akin to that of doctors, lawyers, and engineers, who had
recently tightened their training and job qualification process. As Marjorie
Murphy argues in her history of American teacher unions, this attempt to
professionalize did not raise the occupation to the status of a profession, but
it did significantly shape the political character of the teaching force. Selective admissions excluded working-class and ethnic applicants who might
bring with them radical political inclinations and strong ethnic and community allegiances. And the increased years in teacher education furthered the
socialization of prospective teachers into the occupational identity that was
promoted by school administrators. Thus the attempts to professionalize
teaching meant the expanded regulation of those who applied to the occupation and the reshaping of those who entered it. Even as the number of teaching jobs increased and liberal laws welcomed teachers from all backgrounds,
the increased requirements for the job prohibited the majority of New Yorkers from considering teaching.[12]

If teaching remained an ambiguous occupational option for working-
class and ethnic-minority candidates, it was an increasingly popular career
option for middle-class white women. Teaching first became identified as
"women's work" in the mid-nineteenth century as part of the common
school movement to institutionalize local public school systems. Nineteenth-
century school reformers such as Horace Mann and Henry Barnard saw
women as attractive candidates for teaching because they demanded, or
could be presented with, lower salaries than men, thereby keeping the costs

of local school systems down. Even with these restrictions, middle-class women flocked to teaching because it was consistently the single occupation that offered educated women the hope for financial independence and a meaningful life's work. In 1870 two-thirds of American teachers were female, and by 1900 over three-quarters of the teaching force was female, and in urban areas upward of 80%. After 1870, teaching was among the top five employers of women nationwide, and during the 1920s teaching was the second leading occupation for women, behind only domestic service. For foreign-born women and their daughters, teaching was the fifth leading occupation, and the seventh leading occupation for black women, most of whom worked in the separate black schools of the South.[13]

In New York in the 1920s, teaching paid more than the feminized occupations of nursing and clerical work, and even more than many unskilled men's jobs. In the mid-1920s, the median annual salary for elementary school teachers in New York City was $2,800 when two-thirds of all New York City families earned less than $2,500 a year. Women teachers in New York City schools in the 1920s also enjoyed unprecedented employment benefits. They were hired from separate eligibility lists that paired men and women equally: School principals were restricted to choosing from a list of the 10 best men and the 10 best women, thus ostensibly preventing them from preferring men over women. Unlike most cities and virtually all rural school districts, New York City women teachers earned equal pay with their male colleagues, and they were guaranteed employment after marriage and childbirth.[14]

Teaching was also presented in promotional literature and popular culture as an ideal, almost glamorous job for women that was more prestigious and exciting than nursing or clerical work. Teaching was given a kind of professional veneer that separated it from other work and that characterized the ideal woman teacher as a paragon of modernity. An elementary teacher reported on in a New York City newspaper in 1920 was the epitome of a modern girl who was a loyal citizen, socially conscious, *and* intelligent: "Miss Branham teaches, saves lives, writes a thesis, then [goes] off to campaign for [the] labor party and against [the] Russian blockade." According to teacher education promotional literature and textbooks and the popular press, the ideal teacher was a patriot, a creative volunteer, a producer of order, and an emotionally stable and satisfied middle-class white woman.[15]

A cartoon called "Spring Vacation" reproduced in a national education journal in the mid-1920s highlighted the social difference between the ideal woman teacher and other female white-collar employees. A young and well-dressed blonde woman identified as a schoolteacher strides across the page with a suitcase in one hand, a travel timetable under her arm, and a breezy smile on her face. Left behind are "the rest of us"—a group of surly and harassed women tending to their work as secretary, librarian, waitress, sales clerk, telephone operator, nurse, and drafter. They are exhausted, frazzled, and worn down by their work. Three are literally bound to their work by a ball and chain around the ankle. All seven glare at the sprightly teacher and think that she is "pretty soft." The message was that of all the jobs open to women, teaching was the best paid and best rewarded. Furthermore, teaching required a certain level of class collateral: The well-dressed woman off to vacation in foreign spots was a cultured middle-class woman, her blonde hair betraying a Northern European background, her strong stride and straight back indicating self-confidence bred from a solid native-born American family. This was the ideal woman teacher, notably different from her dark-haired, ragged, ill-tempered, and presumably lower-class friends in less professional occupations.[16]

But this ideal was difficult to attain in city school systems, causing teacher educators great anxiety. Even given the tightened entrance requirements to the occupation, some educators worried about the social qualities of the nation's teachers. Lotus Coffman's 1911 study of the "social composition" of the occupation shocked educators with the finding that the typical American teacher was a young woman from a working-class or lowly farmer background. Related research on the social and cultural background of students in teachers colleges gloomily described future teachers as poorly educated, narrow-minded, and, in the larger cities, increasingly from immigrant backgrounds. A study in the late 1920s confirmed that one-quarter of the students at teacher training schools around the country had foreign-born parents. Since school was one of the main agencies for transferring American culture to students, teachers carried the responsibility for "modifying the old cultures" by teaching common American values. If teachers themselves were part of that "old culture," the argument went, they might have trouble doing this. As one educator complained in 1925, "the racial and family background of many teachers is such that they are not prepared to transmit the best American political and social ideals to the children under their care."[17]

This situation was magnified in New York City, the immigrant capital of the nation. Since the turn of the century, teaching had been to second-generation Irish American women what domestic service had been to the first generation: an easily accessible occupation that promised economic stability. But by the 1920s, young Jewish men and women were competing with Irish Americans for teaching jobs for some very specific economic reasons. Of all immigrant groups, Jewish children had fared the best in school, and by the 1920s they had one of the highest rates of secondary school attendance. But educated Jewish New Yorkers in the 1920s faced so many hiring quotas in private businesses that one contemporary observer estimated that they were excluded from 90% of the office jobs in New York City. Private universities also had Jewish quotas for undergraduate and graduate enrollment, but the public city colleges were open to all, and Jewish New Yorkers entered those institutions at rates higher than those of any other ethnic group. Because the New York City Board of Education had no Jewish quotas, teaching became one of the few occupations open to educated Jewish New Yorkers. Although estimates vary, as many as one-third of the new recruits to teaching in the early 1920s were Jewish, increasing to almost two-thirds by 1930. Historian Ruth Markowitz estimated that in the years between the two world wars, almost three-quarters of the women students at the city's teacher training schools were Jewish when Jewish students constituted less than 4% of male and female teacher education students in the nation at large.[18]

Other cultural characteristics caused concern among nativist observers of schools. At the teacher training schools in both Queens and Brooklyn in 1928, more than two-thirds of the freshman class lived in homes where parents were foreign-born, and one-half of the students spoke two or more languages other than English. At a training school in Queens, a researcher noted that the combination of foreign parentage and foreign language spoken in the home raised the "high probability" that three-quarters of the students were likely to speak with a foreign accent. Less than one-fifth of these students had lived outside of New York City, and none had lived outside the industrial Northeast. This urban provincialism, the researcher noted, narrowed prospective teachers' understanding of the broader world and introduced the "real danger that the culture of the city will become something essentially different from that of most of the other parts of the United States." Implicit in these concerns was the assumption that the culture of urban ethnic immigrants would derail the creation of a prestigious teaching profession. The local city-dweller from a foreign background was viewed as backward and provincial, as well as potentially imbued with radical political ideas—not like the ideal teacher, who was presumably well versed in "American political and social ideals."[19]

Educators' concern with the personal makeup of teachers reached new heights in the 1920s with educational research on teachers' "personality traits." Teacher educators drew on the new field of psychology to emphasize that teachers' personality development was as important a variable in the job as teaching methods or content. In the period after World War I, the most intimate parts of teachers' lives became subject to systematic surveillance and evaluation. Under scrutiny were family backgrounds, grades and rates of absenteeism in high school and college, physical health, appearance, speech, age, extracurricular activities, reading habits, hobbies, handwriting, marital status, and family responsibilities. Researchers developed and administered tests that evaluated "mental keenness," "sympathy," "public opinion," and emotional history. A flurry of studies were conducted evaluating the intelligence of students in teachers colleges, using the new intelligence tests developed for army recruits during the war. Overwhelmingly, the test results agreed that the most significant determinant for effective teaching had less to do with intelligence or academic training and more to do with "personality traits." Or as one researcher worded it: Those personal qualities called "temperamental makeup" were more important than "intellectual makeup." The personality of the teacher determined success or failure in the classroom, argued a Vermont superintendent in 1919. He concluded that "good teaching personality is the outward expression of genuine, refined, sympathetic and virile manhood and womanhood." Other critics of the occupation observed that good teaching required a continually positive outlook, a generous spirit, selflessness, sympathy, judgment, self-control, and enthusiasm. The most successful teachers, they agreed, "are those who take a happy attitude toward their work of teaching. They fail to see the drudgery of a necessary task, and always radiate enough sunshine about an assigned lesson to encourage pupils to want to study and prepare it."[20]

In teachers colleges, in professional journals and the public press, and in their very own school buildings, teachers were advised and admonished about their dress, way of speaking, and social habits. The teacher was nothing less than a public figure with public responsibilities, argued Herbert Hoover, who proclaimed that a teacher literally could not separate teaching from "daily walk and conversation." Constantly in the public arena, the teacher was "peculiarly a public character under the most searching scrutiny of watchful and critical eyes." The teacher's life, Hoover concluded, was "an open book." The force of these social pressures fell hardest on teachers in rural and small-town communities, where some teachers' contracts included commitments to refrain from smoking cigarettes or drinking alcohol, loitering in public places, or wearing colors that were too bright or dresses that were too short, and to abstain from dancing, dating, or falling in love. Some districts even admonished teachers to sleep regularly and eat carefully, to be cheerfully involved in Sunday School work, and generally to be a "willing servant" of the school board and the townspeople.[21]

But even in cities, the emphasis on teachers' personal attributes made teachers' habits subject to public discussion and monitoring. There was a direct relation between teachers' poor behavior and the low prestige of the occupation, argued Chicago's superintendent, who told his city's principals that the cause of the public's slow acceptance of teaching as a profession was due less to weak classroom performance and more to the "ungroomed appearance of teachers." Back in New York, a teachers' employment agency rejected applicants who were "giddily attired" with bobbed hair, short skirts, and excessive makeup. At the New York Training School for Teachers in the early 1920s, a "courtesy campaign" was conducted to emphasize the value of "politeness and civility at all times in the life of the teacher." As students walked to class, they saw a series of mottos and slogans on politeness projected on a corridor wall from a timed slide projector. Student teachers and their faculty prepared a "politeness-play" and heard a lecture on the subject by two professors from Columbia Teachers College. One of those professors later wrote that one peculiar disadvantage of the urban teacher training school was that students were not continually under the control of the institution and were not constantly living with the correct "professional ideals." They were potentially contaminated by the beliefs and cultures of the outside world—and by the particularly poisonous world of urban street culture.[22]

New York City teachers were also evaluated for promotion by a rating scale that included both personal and professional behavior. Principals made annual inspections of teachers and completed a standard rating form with categories of evaluation for instruction, discipline, routine completion of official paperwork, and personal appearance and professional attitude. Teachers were rated satisfactory or unsatisfactory on their personal presentation in the class, including their use of voice, cheerfulness, courtesy, self-control, initiative and demonstrated leadership, tact, and sympathy. The category of professional attitude reflected just as much emphasis on personal behavior. The professional teacher was punctual, cooperative, and took part in volunteer activities and other activities for "self-improvement." The professional teacher was also one who rated well on "loyalty" as well as the care of children. Professional and personal attributes were hardly distinguishable for the teacher, and both were subject to inspection by the employer.[23]

If ethnicity, class, and social behavior were threats to professional stature, the gender composition of teaching presented another problem. An "excess" of women, some educators argued, kept teacher salaries low, threatened to endanger the masculinity of young male students, and undercut the potential professional status of the occupation. Social commentators of the period argued that male teachers were in particular demand in the feminized elementary school because they would present a more masculine spirit to the classroom—a spirit that was described as benefiting only young boys and not girls. The ideal male teacher was promoted in popular literature as "virile, versatile, and accomplished," and his scholarly attributes and social prestige were emphasized. Men teachers with strong personalities were active contributors to the "machinery of life" and to the professional status of teaching.[24]

Throughout the 1920s, the New York City Board of Education decried the "shortage" of men teachers, particularly in the high schools and all-male elementary and high schools. The perceived necessity that men teach boys led the board of education to hire male teachers from outside the city rather than local women: In 1921 60 of the 173 men teachers at the all-male Stuyvesant High School in Manhattan commuted from other boroughs and two neighboring states. In May 1921 the board of education held a "man's teacher day" when school superintendents addressed high school boys about the benefits of entering the teaching profession. In New York and other city school systems, the development of the teachers' pension in the early twentieth century was explicitly designed to attract young "family men" to a committed career in teaching, replacing the predominantly female teaching force that was incorrectly described as shifting and impermanent. Pensions, like other benefits, held the added attraction of creating social stability and professional commitment among teachers, thereby appeasing and deradicalizing the teaching force.[25]

While men were praised as professionals, women teachers were seen as merely fulfilling their "natural" attribute of caring for children. Mid-nineteenth-century common school reformers had supported the feminization of the teaching force by arguing that the school should be an extension of the idealized middle-class family and home, with the gentle female supervising a flock of children, all under the command of a male authority figure in the principal's office. Women teachers could be, as the founder of the German kindergarten, Frederick Froebel argued, like "a mother made conscious." Economics and culture reinforced each other: That school boards could pay women less than men indicated that women were less interested in money than men and thus had less professional drive. This construction of women's lack of interest in material rewards furthered the image of women teachers as missionaries and their interest in teaching as a calling that demanded personal strength and emotional commitment, not financial or professional interests. The nineteenth-century educator Catherine Beecher essentially justified her campaign for the hiring of women teachers by distinguishing their objectives as different from, and far superior to, the earning of money: The ideal teacher worked "not for money, not for influence, nor for humour, nor for ease, but with the simple, single purpose of doing good."[26]

Over time, the image of the moral and ever-patient woman teacher grew to be central to the cultural identity of the occupation and counterpoised the increasing impersonality of expanding urban school bureaucracies. In both popular culture and educational dialogue of the 1920s, the woman teacher was portrayed as "naturally" maternal, caring, and patient, and as having a greater interest in personal satisfaction than in financial reward. Local teacher journals and the popular press were rich with poetry and stories that glorified the woman teacher who labored her life away for the benefit of children. In the 1926 annual report of the Brooklyn Teachers' Association, a woman teacher was eulogized with just such an image of the self-sacrificing and devoted teacher:

> Fifty years a toiling teacher
> Many pangs she knew!
> Sacrificed a happy fireside!
> Asked for pleasures few!
> Proudly she, when duty beckoned,
> Rendered service true![27]

The public image of the nurturing female elementary teacher undergirded many women's decisions to enter the occupation. "I have forgotten everything the schools ever taught me," a New Yorker remembered about her childhood in a poor immigrant district of early-twentieth-century Manhattan. "But the glamour of the lady teachers, shining on the East Side World, I shall never forget." In the immigrant district of Brownsville in Brooklyn in the same period, the local elementary school was the central interest of the entire neighborhood, which held up the school principal as the highest authority and discussed each woman teacher with "the minute detail a jeweler devotes to a watch." To Brownsville residents, school represented "a glorious future that would rescue it from want, deprivation, and ugliness." Jane Addams observed that poor city children in Chicago used the word "teacher" as a synonym for women of a certain gentry manner and dress.[28]

Even for those women teachers who entered teaching for practical reasons, many articulated a personal vision in their occupational goals. One retired teacher believed she was drawn to teaching by a feeling that a teacher could change students, "that you could instill some of the attributes that you wanted them to grow up with." Another retired teacher remembered that she was interested in "finding out what made a youngster tick," adding "If I hadn't loved teaching, I wouldn't have gone into it." A student's memory of her elementary teacher in the 1920s also indicated the way in which some women teachers approached their job as a caring and generous relationship with children that included giving students books, crayons, praise, and affection. A former student in New York City in the 1920s recalled the warmth and caring of one elementary teacher: "She would hug me and take me in her arms; she would nurture me." Such teachers incorporated into their personal lives and professional practices the public expectation of women teachers as nurturing and generous social servants.[29]

But when many young women and men finally became teachers, they were often alarmed to find a disjuncture between their image of the generous and caring teacher and the hard work and often menial conditions of the job. In Polish immigrant Anzia Yezierska's fictionalized account of her own teaching experience in New York City schools, the heroine reflected ambivalently on her new job teaching other immigrant children in a school located on the same crowded ghetto street where she had grown up selling herring. For Sara, the role of the teacher lost much of the glamour and inspiration that it had carried when she was a little girl longing for attention from the "superior creature," the teacher. She wondered:

> Now I was the teacher. Why didn't I feel as I had supposed this superior creature felt? . . . Not one of the teachers around me had kept the glamour. They were just peddling their little bit of education for a living, the same as any pushcart peddler.[30]

In fact, what teacher education and the employment process failed to make known to potential job applicants was that teachers were overworked, tired people just like anybody else and that they shared the common public's health problems and personality quirks. Teacher advocates blamed large classes and stuffy, poorly ventilated classrooms for the high rates of chronic invalidism among city teachers. Some studies showed that while the intensity of teaching might not cause mental disorders, it may have hastened some cases of mental instability. A 1931 study of former New York City teachers in mental hospitals found that, at the very least, teachers were no healthier than the average citizen and that they suffered their share of insanity in the family, sexually related problems (including illegitimate children, broken engagements, failed marriages, and sexually transmitted diseases), and excessive work and financial anxieties. Over half of the institutionalized teachers were economically "marginal," or barely self-supporting.[31]

The emphasis on personal attributes permitted educators to evaluate teachers by who they were, not by what they did, and to develop entrance requirements that were thinly veiled efforts to regulate the entry of certain types of applicants. Ethnicity, gender, and class assumptions were used to measure teachers against a standard image of the ideal "professional" teacher who was a composite paragon of middle-class, Anglo American, and gendered values. In a cartoon in the *National Education Association Research Bulletin* in the fall of 1926 the ideal teacher was portrayed just this way. A dozen young women and men who are recent high school graduates stand at "Life's Crossroads," deciding to take one of two paths. They are, as the caption reads "the nation's most promising youth." All the figures are white and well dressed, the young women wearing neat dresses and sporting bobbed hair, the young men standing tall in suits. The young people face two possible paths for their future career: One path leads up to a clean, stately building standing alone on a hill and identified as a teachers college. Only three lone characters far in the distance march up the steps to that future. The second path leads to other professions and occupations, and meanders up a hill to a veritable city of colleges, hospitals, factories, and shops. This path is jammed with young people, presumably flocking to the excitement of the professions. The cartoon is a comment on the depressing state of teaching, which competed with *all* the other occupations for the best-qualified candidates. And according to the cartoon, there was only one kind of qualified candidate: young white high school graduates, neatly dressed, alert, and cultured—and without doubt Anglicized and middle-class individuals.[32]

The emphasis on the individual attributes and personality of both male and female teachers decontextualized teachers' work from the broader labor processes and organization of the school. Teachers were taught to see occupational problems as the result of a deficient personality, not a poor school organization. Those teachers who faced problems in the classroom were urged not to look to their colleagues or administrators for help with their work, but to look inside themselves, and certainly not to complain to a local union organizer about problems at work. It is not surprise that in the 1920s—a period of intense occupational growth, increasing occupational problems, and worsening working conditions—school administrators promoted a notion of teacher professionalism that kept teachers focused on their own personal characteristics and not on the nature of their working conditions.

DIVISIONS IN THE STAFF ROOM

School employees brought their own stereotypes and ideologies to work with them, helping to design the interior relations, personal dynamics, and working environment within schools. Teachers and administrators learned about informal shortcuts in the system to prevent or discourage some teachers from working in certain schools and to encourage the employment of other teachers. Thus within the formal framework of official employment rights and privileges rested a maze of interpersonal politics, informal proscriptions, sanctions, and prejudices. The undercutting of official regulations most directly affected those teachers for whom the policies had been designed to protect—women, ethnic minorities, and African Americans.

Once graduated from training school or college, applicants applied for a teacher's license and took a lengthy written examination on academic and pedagogical subjects, including educational theory, child psychology, and classroom management. High school teachers were also examined on their subject specialty. Next was an oral examination before the board of examiners to evaluate the applicant's use of language, the evaluation of the teaching of a model lesson, a medical exam, and a personal interview with a member of the board of examiners. Successful applicants were placed on a citywide eligibility list in order of the evaluation of their performance on the tests to wait for appointment to a school. Principals hiring new teachers were supposed to choose the top name on the list and interview the candidate.[33]

While the official hiring process ostensibly prevented principals from choosing teacher applicants on anything but their qualifications, there was room for maneuvering within the school bureaucracy. For example, principals were required to choose candidates from an eligibility list of the most recently certified candidates. But principals were able to work around this regulation by appointing substitute teachers and later working them into the school, stalling an appointment until the desired teacher rose to the top of the list, or threatening teachers not to join certain staffs. Principals were rarely forced to hire a teacher whom they did not like.[34]

Community networks bolstered this informal system of favoritism. In New York, Irish American men and women had traditionally settled in community-based civil service jobs, including police work and public school teaching, relying on the Irish American political machine to make appointments. Local Irish American political networks existed well into the twentieth century, even with the growth of other ethnic communities. Well through the 1920s, Irish American strongholds on local school boards and within the board of education assured many Irish American applicants jobs in the schools and eased the entry of a new teacher of Irish heritage. At schools under the control of Irish Catholic superintendents, Irish Catholic teachers had the advantage of sharing a common cultural base with their superiors. One Irish American teacher found this to work to her professional advantage: Her friendship with her superintendent, a former Jesuit priest, was partially based on his visits to her music class, where they sang Christmas carols together.[35]

Connections also worked for those job applicants from *outside* the power structure. A black teacher applicant who had community links or who was from a visibly well-off family might have had better chances of working her way into the system. At PS 122 in Queens, for example, the principal hired the daughter of the local black undertaker, a visible and respectable member of the community. And after Isabel Ross's success as the first Jewish teacher in a predominately Italian American and Irish American school in Brooklyn, the principal hired two of her Jewish friends, commenting with surprise that she never knew that Jewish teachers could be so good. Teacher applicants learned that it was inside personal connections that opened the door to a good job, not one's qualifications.[36]

Other practices allowed administrators to undercut the color-blind hiring procedures. Many black teacher applicants had migrated to New York from the South, and some school principals listened for southern accents on telephone interviews and scanned teachers' resumes for evidence of race. Sadie Delany, the first black domestic science teacher in New York, was the daughter of the nation's first black Episcopal bishop, a graduate of private schools and of Columbia Teachers College. But even she needed to use her wit and wiles to earn a job in the New York City public school system, investing in speech lessons to erase her southern accent. She intentionally skipped her job interview with the school principal, sent him a letter pretending that her absence was due to a scheduling mix-up, and showed up on the first day of class ready to work. Sadie suspected that, even as a light-skinned black woman from a middle-class background, she would have been immediately denied the job on first sight.[37]

Ethnic diversity in the teaching staff was also undermined by some school programs that were designed intentionally to promote ethnic homogeneity. William Maxwell, superintendent of New York City schools from 1898 to 1916, promoted community schools where teachers and students came from similar backgrounds. In predominantly Jewish communities, such as the Lower East Side of Manhattan and the Brownsville area of Brooklyn, possibly half of all teachers were Jewish in the 1920s. In Harlem as well, the increased black population furthered the creation of schools staffed primarily by black teachers, especially when white teachers increasingly viewed their appointment to Harlem as punishment. In 1930 the board of education introduced experimental classes in Hebrew at two Brooklyn high schools that were both run by Jewish principals and located in Jewish communities. A campaign to introduce Italian into the New York City schools was supported by the board of education less for the sake of diversity than in hopes that the classes might appease rough Italian American boys. The creation of culturally homogeneous school staffs in select communities ran smack against the intentions of earlier school reformers who had replaced the local ward system of schooling with a powerful centralized school management. One of the major publicly stated objectives of the new centralized school system was to hire and promote teachers based on objective examinations and performance assessments, not on personal connections. Yet in practice, school administrators promoted ethnic divisions where it seemed politically expedient.[38]

Discriminatory hiring practices for men and women teachers were also publicly acknowledged and defended by the board of education against challenges by women teachers. The bitter irony of the barriers that faced women teachers was that the occupation was numerically dominated by women. If gender inequities were going to occur, one might think they would be directed against men in the same way that women were traditionally prevented from entering male-dominated fields. In elementary schools in particular, the cultural emphasis on the maternal teacher might have privileged women over men. Yet this was not the case. Although many of the gender-equity personnel policies that were introduced to the occupation in this period did improve women teachers' employment rights, many of those same policies were systematically undercut through local practice. In 1910 and 1918 New York City women teachers sued the board for maintaining a separate male and female list for teacher and principal appointments. The eligibility lists were divided by type of license and on the basis of sex, under the board's argument that one common list would unfairly discriminate against men, who constituted only 15% of all teachers in the system. Women teachers complained that principals tended to hire all the candidates from the men's list before turning to the list of qualified women. Furthermore, even if men and women were hired in turn, the very existence of the list was discriminatory because there were so many fewer males than females. State courts upheld the board's discretion to determine whether a position could go to a man or a woman by noting the obvious need for male teachers in the school system.[39]

Salaries were equal between men and women in the same job category only, and the New York City system offered dozens of different job categories, or levels of teaching with different salary scales. Women dominated those positions at the bottom rung of the salary scale. Elementary school teachers, for example, earned about two-thirds of high school teachers' salaries, and 90% of the city's elementary teachers were women. Sixty percent of secondary teachers were women, but this was a far smaller pool than the number of elementary teachers: In 1927 fewer than 3,000 women taught in New York high schools, compared to 9,000 who taught for lower salaries in elementary and junior high schools. In secondary schools, where most men teachers worked, the salary scale began a full $400 above elementary teachers' salary, and principals' salaries began at over twice that of teachers. Other positions dominated by women earned less than high school or junior high school teachers, including school secretary and positions in kindergarten, special education, home economics, and elementary vocational education.[40]

In the early 1920s, teachers at the Manhattan Trade School for Girls, the only vocational high school for girls in the city and a school where women teachers dominated the staff, claimed sex discrimination before the state's commissioner of education because the salary scale for teachers in vocational schools for girls was an average of $200 less than that for teachers at vocational schools for boys. In his two decisions upholding the differential, the commissioner noted that different pay scales for the sexes were allowed if the work was different and distinct. Because different subjects were taught at the two schools, differential pay was justified.[41]

Even judicial decisions that supported women could be undermined. A

1904 legal decision forced the board of education to continue to employ women teachers after marriage, but many principals made clear their disapproval of married women teachers. They joined a chorus of objecting voices across the country that condemned the steady increase of working married women. By 1930 almost one-third of all American women in the labor force were married. In school districts where married women were not prohibited from employment, they flooded the market, and New York was no exception. Historian Ruth Markowitz estimates that well over half of New York City women teachers in the interwar years were married. A selective study of one-third of New York City women teachers in the mid-1920s found that about 20% were married, although since the study asked respondents to report the information to a public agency, some may have denied their marital state because of public disapproval of their marital status. In educational and popular writings around the country, married women teachers were criticized for alleged poor work records, for high absentee rates, and for neglecting their familial responsibilities. Critics characterized them as immoral for leaving their responsibilities at home, as selfish for taking a job merely to earn money for frivolities, and as dangerous for the profession because they kept salaries low so that men continued to find other, more profitable occupations. This final remarkable argument rested on the logic that women teachers commanded the power to prevent the board of education from raising their salaries. Critics also charged all women teachers with undermining the profession by working for only a short term until marriage and motherhood sent them home, where presumably they stayed. In fact, they did not stay home: Markowitz found that in New York, almost 90% of those who applied for maternity leave returned to the classroom after their leave.[42]

In spite of protections, many married women teachers were denied appointment. One applicant attested that the physician appointed by the board of education to examine prospective teachers failed her simply because of her marital status. She remembered: "He told me I was sick—not because I had some trouble. . . . It was just because I was married and that's why I should not be teaching." The female principal at an elementary school in Queens announced publicly that she disapproved of married women teachers. One day, she called all the teachers into a special meeting to explain the reasoning behind her position:

> She said: I don't want to make any bones about it. I do not approve of married women teaching. I don't see how you can stand in front of a class after you've slept with a *man* the night before.[43]

Married women teachers in both elementary and secondary schools were also discouraged from moving up in the system by family pressures and social tensions faced by working women in the 1920s. "The day has not come," wrote one college-educated woman in 1928, "when the married woman who works for any cause other than direct economic necessity may escape the criticism of her friends, her community, and often her own family." Marriage or family responsibilities might discourage a woman from completing the time-consuming coursework and exam required for administrative positions. One New York City teacher remembered how the family duties of a woman colleague prevented even the consideration of upward mobility:

> I had a good friend whose husband was a salesman and he was away a lot of the time. When he was home she needed to stay home with him, so she never had the time to take courses to be an administrator.[44]

But single women teachers, too, faced barriers to career advancement in the occupation. Women numerically dominated the occupation, but only in the "lower strata of the upper crust" commented a contemporary critic. Few New York City women actually reached the higher echelons of administration, and those who did were principals of elementary schools, girls' high schools, or assistant principals in charge of annex buildings and training schools—all positions that paid less than coeducational or all-male high schools. Gender discrimination was interwoven in both the structural organization of the school system and in informal practices and expectations. Women were discouraged from advancement in the school system by a range of informal "old-boy" networks of administrators who controlled the appointment and promotion process. Not only did many teachers share a common belief that advancement within the system was based on political patronage and favoritism, but women teachers suspected that men administrators undermined their chances at career mobility. School bureaucracy, observed one woman critic, created an "inclined plane" where men governed "the grade and the scale."[45]

Women may have had a better chance of achieving upward mobility in the school system if they were single and lived alone or with their families. Margaret Jamer, who became an assistant principal after 10 years of teaching, attributed her professional success to her living situation.

> I had a mother who did everything for me . . . [she] prepared dinner for me every night and watched over me like a fairy princess. Some of the teachers had to do an awful lot for themselves. I think some of the mothers of the teachers went out to work so that some teachers . . . had to go home and cook or clean.[46]

But most single women teachers were also deterred from advancement in the school system because even they had family responsibilities—a concept that was lost on most critics who accused single women of wanting to work merely for the fun of it. One 1927 survey estimated that almost three-fourths of all New York City women teachers—both married and unmarried—had one or more dependents. This corresponded with a national finding that between 1888 and 1923 over 90% of wage-earning women contributed at least part of their income to family support. Many unmarried women teachers lived with parents, sharing family expenses and often taking on such responsibilities as the support of a sibling's education, an ailing parent, or household upkeep. Many women chose elementary teaching specifically because it required two years (and after 1923, one year) less training than high school teaching, thus allowing them to begin helping their families that much earlier. Some teachers' biographies can only suggest the conflicting family dynamics at play. Isabel Ross's older brother, who was a high school principal, encouraged her to take the administrators' exam. But Isabel, who lived at home with her widowed mother, lost her "eagerness" to prepare for the test after she was hurt in an accident. Isabel knew she could pass the exam: "But it meant reading a lot and giving up on social activities and maybe I just didn't want to. I don't know, the whole desire just left."[47]

Of course many women might have claimed that career advancement would draw them out of the classroom and into an administrative office—a job change that may not necessarily have appealed to them. But such a change apparently appealed to men, who rose out of the classroom into administrative positions at a far higher rate than women. Furthermore, one's career choices within the occupation significantly determined income. Thus the barriers to advancement that were presented to women limited their earnings, as well as their professional authority within the school system.

At one level in city schools men and women teachers were in an unusually egalitarian situation. High school teaching staffs may have had the most gender-integrated occupation in the nation, as men and women worked together in equal or near-equal numbers, earning the same salary and coordinating their work as colleagues. About two-thirds of all high school teachers were women. Gender ratios varied within departments: Men dominated in math and the sciences, and women were predominant in English, language, art, and social science departments. But in single-sex girls' schools women teachers were preferred to teach all subjects, including math and science, and men dominated the staffs only at all-boy academic and vocational schools. And even in those single-sex schools, like the academic all-boys Stuyvesant High School, where only 10% of the staff was female, men and women still worked together on an equal footing. Women high school teachers remembered collegiality and friendship with their male colleagues that was highly unusual for most sex-segregated work in the period. At New Utrecht High School in Brooklyn in the mid-1920s, a woman science teacher remembered that:

Many of the science teachers were men. In physics and chemistry the majority were men. But in biology we were evenly divided. We were well mixed. We had men working with women on an equal basis. We all had to take the same examination. We all got the same salary. There was no way the men could do better than the women because he was a man.[48]

Many secondary teachers also joined together across the city in subject-area professional associations. Subject associations such as the Italian Teachers Association and a variety of science associations gave high school teachers common professional and social networks, and offered professional educational activities such as field trips, lectures, and reading groups.

But ironically, the conditions that unified men and women in secondary schools disunited the teaching force as a whole. Women secondary teachers had a completely different working experience from their sisters who taught in elementary schools. Separate salary scales, unique job descriptions, and different public expectations left women elementary and secondary teachers with almost nothing in common. Secondary teachers were four-year college graduates and might be more likely to come from a higher class background than their elementary teacher friends who were graduates of the two- and three-year teacher training schools. Class differences between elementary and secondary teachers might only be furthered by the higher salaries in secondary teaching. These differentiations were critical in the continung disunity of all New York City teachers.

Schisms between teachers were furthered by ethnic divisions within school staffs. Many Jewish teachers were the first non-Christians that their colleagues had met, and they encountered a range of treatment from exceptionalism to exclusion. Isabel Ross was the first Jewish teacher hired into a staff that was predominately Irish Catholic, many of them senior women teachers as old as her mother. Teachers socialized by their religious and ethnic background, leaving Isabel stranded at her own lunch table in the teachers' lounge. Jewish teachers often worked where there was a common assumption of Christian cultural knowledge, and they heard Christian readings at daily assemblies, learned and taught Christian songs, and produced Christmas pageants. Gentile educators stereotyped Jewish teachers as being "good with money" or especially good at commercial or bookkeeping courses. Many Jewish teachers often sensed that their principal or assistant principal disapproved of and disliked them, even if they never betrayed it outwardly.[49]

Teachers from immigrant backgrounds were also victims of less subtle discrimination. The revived American nationalist crusades of the postwar era were notably anti-Semitic and anti-immigrant. In schools across the nation after World War I, legislators passed resolutions affirming the use of

American texts by American authors, teachers were forced to sign loyalty oaths as a condition of employment, and educators and politicians promoted the school as a "militant protagonist" of "American ideals." The infamous Lusk Commission in New York State investigated charges of teacher disloyalty between 1919 and 1924. Organized for the purpose of rooting Bolshevism out of the state's schools, the Commission focused on teachers who refused to sign loyalty oaths during the war. Of the 30 New York City teachers who were investigated, most were Jewish, and the three teachers who were fired were Jewish. Henry Linville, president of the recently formed Teachers Union, charged that the blurring of lines between "disloyalty" and "conduct unbecoming a teacher" allowed many teachers to be fired for underlying anti-Semitic motives. "If a teacher happens to be a Jew, and a Socialist, and to be personally disliked by an official, the technique of 'indirection' takes care of it all through the euphemism of 'conduct unbecoming a teacher.'" [50]

The authorization of Jewish teachers' unpaid leave for religious holidays reflects some of the ambiguities about Jewish teachers' activism in the schools. When Jewish teachers stayed out of work on religious holidays, the board of education transferred non-Jewish teachers to substitute for the day. Teachers who were assigned to substitute complained that principals used the assignment to punish them or that only new and inexperienced teachers were chosen. Substituting teachers also blamed Jewish teachers for causing the problem in the first place. That Jewish teachers served as the backbone of the Teachers Union worked to stereotype teacher activism as something "Jewish," contributing to ethnic divisions within the teaching force and isolating the Union. [51]

Black teachers, too, experienced continued alienation within an occupation that was allegedly color-blind but that was in fact deeply divided by race. Although barely 1% of the city's teaching force was African American in 1930, the NAACP consistently held up New York City as the model of integration in its schools, noting that those 300 black teachers were proportionally twice the number of black teachers in Chicago, Cleveland, or Los Angeles. The black journal The Crisis praised New York for such a diffusion of black teachers throughout the system that black teachers were more likely to teach white children than black. Teaching in liberal cities such as New York was only one of the many occupations opened up to black women by the world war and the "collapsing of racial barriers," lauded a writer for the journal of the National Urban League in 1923. [52]

But black teachers who survived the interview process faced considerable trouble inside their schools. Most black teachers were assigned to schools in Harlem, primarily because of the board of education's concern about white parents complaining about black teachers. In Harlem, black teachers faced the worst working conditions in the city, including the most overcrowded and outdated school buildings, and students with the most challenging social, familial, and economic backgrounds.[53]

In predominantly white schools, black teachers were plagued by the same prejudices that harassed their students. The first black teacher at Eastern District High School was a light-skinned woman from the British Caribbean who had a degree in speech from Columbia University. She taught Shakespeare and had herself written a number of plays. By the account of her colleague in play production, this black teacher was well assimilated into middle-class white culture, with a classical education background and a social circle of white friends. Although this teacher's "wit and talent" as well as her light skin color and assimilated education and cultural interests helped her to be accepted socially by the other teachers in the school, the principal still assigned another teacher to monitor her play practices in the afternoon.[54] At a junior high school in Brooklyn in the early 1930s, even a culturally assimilated black woman teacher was not fully accepted by her colleagues. Isabel Ross, herself an object of ethnic stereotyping, remembered that even though her black colleague was "very charming, gracious and intelligent" she was a "stranger."

> We didn't know black people. I don't think we had a single black student. She was the only black person and she was strange to the children and she was strange to the adults. We liked her but she had very little to do with us. . . . I don't think many accepted her, although they recognized that she was a ladylike person with charm. But they were not accustomed and they didn't know what to say or do. She was a stranger.[55]

Isabel Ross remembered that this teacher was "unhappy and I know the principal was not happy to have her there."

Black women teachers, like their sisters in other professions, faced a "double task" of home life and work life, wrote Elise Johnson McDougald, the first black graduate of Washington Irving High School and a graduate of Hunter College who followed an unprecedented career in the public schools from elementary teacher to guidance counselor to principal. A black woman in a professional position such as teaching was "struck in the face daily by contempt from the world about her."[56]

CONCLUSION

The entrance requirements to the occupation of teaching doubled as a sorting and socialization mechanism for city school staffs. The prerequisite of secondary and higher education for teachers meant that only the elite few who could afford an education were qualified to be teachers. Teaching was thus a method of upward mobility for those who were already upwardly mobile. Popular images of the professional teacher further narrowed the applicant pool to those candidates who fit that social ideal and who were able and willing to take on the personal responsibility of a job that was billed as both a profession and a volunteeristic mission. Once within the training and employment process, teachers were channeled to certain corners of the occupation based on their gender, class, or ethnic background. Teachers thus learned early in their career that the occupation was organized not by objective values but by local authorities and popular assumptions.

They also learned that the good teacher was an individual on whose character and personality alone rested success and failure at work. The emphasis on the individual personality of the teacher laid the weight of classroom problems on the individual teacher and isolated the responsibility for teacher's work from the social and political context of the school. Teachers were taught to look inward to themselves, not to their colleagues, for help. Nor would colleagues be necessarily helpful in an environment where ethnic and occupational divisions were allowed to flourish. Furthermore, as we shall see in the following chapters, teachers' isolation at work was furthered by stressful working conditions. Trained to focus on their own performance in the classroom, teachers entered an occupation that further distanced them from one another by an intensely busy workday, confusing physical working conditions, and contradictory administrative requirements. From the moment they entered the classroom, teachers were consumed by expansive and complicated curricular expectations that placed on them nothing less than sole responsibility for the academic, social, and cultural education of American youth.

❦ 3 ❧

The Maze of the Curriculum:
The Intensification of Teachers' Work

NOBODY WORKED HARDER than a teacher, argued Isabel Ennis, who taught elementary school in Brooklyn in 1918. She should know. A teacher for 23 years, Ennis was active in local and national classroom teacher associations and had been a leader in the fight to equalize men and women teachers' salaries a decade before. She was a member of the recently formed Teachers' Council advisory group to the board of education and was a diligent watchdog of city and state legislation on salaries, benefits, and promotional practices. In 1918 she was in the middle of a three-year term as the first woman president of the Brooklyn Teachers' Association, the largest local association in the nation. But this was nothing compared to the work of the regular classroom teacher, Ennis asserted, because in demanding modern times, teachers were expected to solve all modern problems. For example, she reminded her colleagues in Brooklyn:

> We are expected to be an arithmetician, a historian, a grammarian, a disciplinarian, a librarian, a sociologist, a penman, an artist, a musician, a model, a moralist, an attendance officer, a clerk, a nurse, a banker, an athlete, a dancer, a supervisor of play and recreation, an engineer, a community-center worker, a farmer, a housekeeper, a medical and sanitary inspector, a host or hostess. We are expected to discover the mentally deficient, the deaf, the feeble-minded, the exceptional and a few more just such. Besides the three R's we are expected to teach thrift, self- government, [and] sex hygiene. . . . We must be resourceful, display initiative, have confidence in ourselves, make our teaching attractive. . . . In fact the demand is so great, teachers hardly know what to slur or what to stress in teaching.[1]

What Ennis saw as a problem was, in fact, what many school reformers envisioned the ideal teacher to be: an energetic and flexible individual who would take on the totality of young peoples' intellectual and personal education. Curriculum reformers in the 1920s proposed that the school educate students in both academic principles and social skills. The dual emphasis on the instruction of children's minds and the socialization of their behaviors was encapsulated in the term *social efficiency,* the name given to the dominant curriculum reform movement of the 1920s. A social efficiency–oriented curriculum was a broad educational plan designed to direct students toward their specific future roles in adult life. Through this curriculum, which was both wide in vision and narrow in objective, schools would eliminate waste and disorder in schools and create appropriately self-directed, or "socially efficient," citizens and workers. The curriculum thus promised to instill order not only in American schools but also in American society.

But teachers experienced the curriculum reform ideas of the 1920s as singularly disorderly. The modern curriculum was a morass of chaotic, contradictory, and poorly managed directives that overwhelmed teachers in a maze of confusing job expectations. Social efficiency–oriented curriculum literature urged teachers to expand their role from pedagogue to social servant, from purveyor of knowledge to a more creative advisor on health, behavior, civics, and culture. Simultaneously, they were expected to follow specific guidelines and to teach to an increasing number of measurements of student accomplishments, including standardized achievement and intelligence tests. Furthermore, however standardized across the city the curriculum was supposed to be, its implementation in local schools was eclectic. According to teachers, the social efficiency curriculum was a particularly inefficient labyrinth of confusing objectives, directives, and resources.

Teachers' experiences with curriculum reform of the 1920s is a case of what Michael Apple has aptly referred to as the "intensification" of teachers' work. Intensification describes the process by which a job is made more demanding by the sheer increase in work expectations. For white-collar workers such as teachers, nurses, lawyers, or managers, intensification refers to chronic work overload in both routine tasks, such as increased paperwork and multiplied bureaucratic regulations, and in expanded job expectations, including increased caseloads and higher performance standards. In the intensified workplace, workers are apt to cut corners and to abandon any creative initiative as they race to speed up their production. Constantly harried and harassed, workers lose control over their own free time and lose opportunities to develop a workplace community with co-workers. Intensification of labor thus increases workers' frustration with their job at the same time that it furthers alienation among workers. For white-collar workers such as teachers, intensification further divides the work force and distracts workers from the potential for collective organization.[2]

The intensification of New York City teachers' work in the 1920s followed just such a pattern. So expansive was the urban teachers' job that they faced a threat of being overwhelmed by a landslide of responsibilities, each deemed vital to the child, the family, and the state. Teachers responded with increasingly bitter complaints, but the intensity of their workplace also distanced them from one another, leaving them to struggle with their working conditions in frustrating isolation. Teachers learned how to cut corners and quietly undermine some of their job requirements, but they were never unified enough to enact significant change in the system. Ironically, then, the broad socialized curriculum of the 1920s, which was designed to enliven the work of teachers and diversify their interactions with students, in actuality silenced them under the weight of its demands.

SOCIAL EFFICIENCY–ORIENTED CURRICULUM IN THE CLASSROOM

Since the turn of the century, educational reformers had promoted the notion of the school as the major socialization agent for an increasingly diverse American population. But in the wake of World War I, a new sense of urgency about American culture inspired school reformers to make additional revisions to the curriculum, further expanding the scope and purpose of the formal education of youth. Because of the serious social challenges of modern urban life, argued reformers, schools could no longer survive on a simple curriculum of intellectual learning. In the electrified Jazz Age, the character and morals of urban youth were dangerously threatened by a decline in family and religious influences, a rise in crime and civic disunity, and other daily urban problems. For adolescents in particular, the vibrant city streets of the postwar era were believed to offer especially dangerous lures, including neighborhood gangs, street gambling, penny arcades, and movie theaters. For immigrant children, educators saw even more dangers. Presumably uneducated in Anglo American civics and Protestant values, often poor and unskilled, the unsocialized immigrant child was considered a threat to the future of modern society.[3]

The presence of such social disorder in city life highlighted what reformers identified as the responsibility of city schools: the systematic education of urban youth *away* from the dangers of the unfettered city streets and *toward* civic and social cohesion. Because the school was a single public institution with trained leadership, facilities, and supplies that was physically located in the midst of blighted urban neighborhoods, social reformers thought that the school should provide the one beam of light connecting the ghetto with the larger society by becoming, literally, a "department store of community service." The National Education Association assigned schools the primary responsibility of arresting the human race from "its present alarming deterioration; if the nation is to be saved, the race is to be saved." In fact, a number of "races" were under discussion. Some reformers such as

Jane Addams, the popular figurehead of urban social reform, described schools as nothing less than the "great savior of the immigrant district." Other reformers more specifically identified the city school as a way to save America *from* immigrants by educating all children in common American civics. This vision of social cohesion was at the heart of the social efficiency–oriented curriculum of the 1920s.[4]

The social efficiency–oriented curriculum was focused most intently on the high schools, where reformers sought to invigorate the academic curriculum that had traditionally dominated adolescent schooling. The leading exemplar for curriculum reform in the 1920s was the National Education Association's Cardinal Principles Report of 1918, a statement by professional educators on the purpose of secondary education in the modern world. The main goal of schooling, the report stated, was not merely the development of academic knowledge but also education for a healthy lifestyle, the productive use of leisure time, the development of ethical character, vocational skills, citizenship, and "worthy home membership." Indeed, the school curriculum must do nothing less than "supplement the homes" in the education of American citizens. The report rode the crest of a wave of curriculum reform that linked the academic course of study with broader social goals. The 1916 National Education Association Report of the Committee on Social Studies revised the traditional history curriculum into a social studies program that included civics, economics, geography, and history, and that emphasized the link between academic study and social behavior. Conceived this way, new high school classes in social studies addressed the civic education of American youth, the values of a democratic and capitalist system, and the responsibility of citizens to support and maintain that system. High school students learned their lessons in civic responsibility when they moved outside the school to help city street cleaners convert an empty lot into a playground or visited a voting booth or City Hall. Many New York City high schools instituted victory gardens during World War I and continued the practice of student gardening on the front lawn or plots adjacent to the school, thereby teaching important values of patriotism as well as principles of self-sufficiency, economy, and agriculture. At Julia Richman High School in Manhattan, social studies teachers designed an experimental course in Industrial History, specifically to interest their working-class students. Because of the absence of an appropriate textbook, teachers and students worked collaboratively on mining sources from local libraries, honing their skills at research while learning about the value of the work in which many of their families were engaged.[5]

Science curricula in the 1920s were also intended to link the study of the academic subject with contemporary social issues, behavior, and values. Indeed, the profound social implications of science were made clear in the spring of 1925, when Tennessee biology teacher John Scopes was arrested and tried on the national stage for breaking a state law that prohibited the teaching of evolution. Across the country, other science educators of the 1920s challenged the confinement of their subject to rigid textbooks. Biology educators promoted a notion of "science for life" in a new curriculum that included hygiene, health, and nature studies. Biology was deemed particularly appropriate for urban adolescents not only because it presented natural phenomena to those who lived in the unnatural city, but also because it taught the values of organic unity to youth who lived among chaos, the principles of adaptation to immigrant youth who had been transplanted, and basic principles of healthy living in an unhealthy city environment. Biology taught students about the natural order and hierarchy of life, as well as how to value cleanliness, to develop healthy (and restrained) attitudes about sex, to respect and value nature, and to believe in natural progress. The hands-on component was particularly critical: Laboratory assignments taught cool scientific processes of examination and evaluation while offering the application of knowledge to the real world. Some New York City science teachers further diversified their classes with field trips to natural sites or the Museum of Natural History, films on scientific subjects, and animal vivisection.[6]

Mathematics educators also advocated a curriculum of practical application in order to "make the teaching of mathematics democratic," as the head of the Mathematics Department at Stuyvesant High School in Manhattan phrased it. Math teachers were encouraged to take up group activities, hands-on learning exercises, and other projects designed to educate students in social skills. The introduction of the slide rule after its use in the army during World War I, along with the expansion of mathematics clubs that specialized in mathematical games, riddles, and relays, further popularized mathematics and made it less abstract and more applicable to daily life. The quantitative character of math allowed for healthy competition among students that taught valuable lessons, according to a New York City math teacher who argued that school contests in mathematics served both as excellent drills and as the opportunity to develop a competitive and enthusiastic school spirit.[7]

Even in a course as traditionally academic as Latin, attempts were made to vitalize the curriculum, particularly after a 1924 study found that all but college preparatory students avoided Latin because they found it boring and irrelevant to modern life. Authors replaced the dry military passages by Caesar with more entertaining selections of myth and cultural history. Latin teachers' guides presented a variety of creative teaching aids, including articles about ancient graffiti discovered at Pompeii, lists of available photographs and slides, and Latin crossword puzzles and word games. A first-year Latin textbook, co-authored by a New York University professor and a teacher at Franklin Lane High School in Brooklyn, included photographs and drawings of Rome with explanatory captions, training in oral pronunciation, lengthy sections on Roman history and culture, and the script for a short comedy set in ancient Rome.[8]

For all the public posturing about the new curriculum in the 1920s, the "learning by doing" approach may have simply been a tactic for dealing with an increasingly diverse pool of high school students who, unlike their predecessors, were not necessarily college-bound or even academically prepared for their grade. For all its intellectual justification, the social efficiency curriculum was essentially a way to make schools more attractive and amenable to a more diverse and presumably less patient audience of adolescents. As historian Edward Krug remarked, the colorful new curriculum of the 1920s may have been less attributable to the Cardinal Principles Report and more a result of the dynamic popularity of Babe Ruth and Charles Lindbergh.[9]

THE TEACHER AS SOCIAL WORKER

The broader social role of the new curriculum intersected with the goals of other reformers who saw the school as the best place to identify, monitor, and treat children's physical and mental illnesses and social problems. Some social reformers promoted the addition of trained staff in schools, including registered nurses, school doctors, and mental health counselors. But in actual practice, the grand goals of health reformers in school fell to teachers, who were expected to take on the monitoring and advising of students' personal well-being. Teachers, in other words, were to adopt the role of the social worker on top of their classroom instruction.

One of the most critical areas of reformers' interest in the schools in the 1920s was student health. Medical tests of draftees in World War I had shown an alarming extent of poor vision and low physical stamina among young American men. Health reformers argued that improper physical hygiene could not only endanger the strength of the nation's defense during the war, but could also threaten the cultural stability of the country in peacetime. The solution was the early education of children in health principles. The healthy child was believed to have fewer absences from school, to be more focused on study, and to be a positive educative influence on friends, parents, siblings, and neighbors. If properly educated, the healthy child would grow up to be a healthy adult who would work harder, shoulder more individual responsibility, and thereby require less community subsidy for hospitals, almshouses, and relief. The health supervision of schoolchildren thus struck at the root problems of both school failure and urban poverty.

Ideally, schools would be regularly staffed by health specialists, but this was easier said than done. Urban schools were not the ideal environment for professional medical practice, and doctors were hardly anxious to hang up their shingle in a city school building with its inadequate services and inefficient administrative processes—not to mention the sheer magnitude of the social and medical problems of urban children. What comprised the normal working conditions of the urban school teacher presented a cacophony of confusion and incompetence to health professionals. A promotional text on health work in American schools sympathetically quoted a British doctor who admitted to feeling "stranded in the strange atmosphere" of his country's schools, where the predominant health problem was not so much "actual illness" as it was the conditions that fostered illness. He may well have spoken for doctors considering work in New York City schools when he characterized his working conditions in urban schools as marked by:

> Dirt, neglect, improper feeding, malnutrition, insufficient clothing, suppurating ears, defective sight, verminous conditions, the impossibility of getting adequate information from the children or a knowledge of their home conditions; and nobody to whom one could give directions or who could help in examining the children. The only means of approaching the parents was to send an official notice that such or such a condition required treatment. My duties began and ceased with endless notifications, and there it all stopped, as very little notice was taken of them.[10]

Few doctors would take on such an assignment. New York City employed the nation's first school medical inspector in 1892, but it never kept its promise to staff the city's schools with an army of health professionals.

In 1902 social reformer Lillian Wald initiated a school nurse program in the schools around her working-class immigrant district in lower Manhattan, and a year later the board of education appropriated funding for 27 nurses to work in city schools and conduct home visits. The nurse seemed to be a promising addition to schools. Nurses were more akin to teachers than doctors were: They were overwhelmingly women and they were prepared to address long-term preventative care issues among the needy and to act as a health educator for teachers, students, and parents. The school nurse was expected to work *with* the teacher and other school staff to create a kind of multiheaded team of instructors in health and hygiene, conducting regular inspections of children and leading regular talks on the importance of fresh air, proper amounts of rest, good posture, principles of infections and contagion, bodily cleanliness, and proper clothing. But financial support for health education was minimal. In 1916 the Board of Education employed only 195 nurses, who were able to examine barely a third of the City's 800,000 school children. By 1932 the number of nurses in *both* public and parochial schools had increased to only 336, or 1 nurse for every 3,000 children.[11]

Given the absence of health professionals in schools, the teacher was expected to take on much of the work of the health educator. Even if only minimally trained in health inspection and education, teachers could apparently do the job, according to one researcher who found that the diligent classroom teacher could discover exactly 72% of all student defects. New York City teachers were expected to take on instruction in general hygiene, from daily inspections of visual acuity to an annual test of vision and hearing, to checking students' hair for lice, to education in the dangers of alcohol and tobacco, principles of antitubercular practices, and good dietary principles. Teachers were also called upon to lead students in a variety of special events in schools designed to heighten health awareness, such as "Tooth Brush Day" in the spring of 1921 when teachers, dentists, and parent groups coordinated educational efforts on dental hygiene. The 1930 course of study for Health Education for the elementary schools outlined teachers' regular obligation to monitor students' seating positions when reading; maintain proper light, temperature, ventilation, and cleanliness in the classroom; allow for well-timed moments of student rest and relaxation; and regularly inspect students for illness and cleanliness of clothing, hair, shoes, and handkerchiefs.[12] A drill for "hygiene position" directed teachers to lead and inspect students in the following exercise:

> Roll up sleeves.
> Extend head backward and turn face from light.
> Draw down collar with hand nearer the window.
> Keep elbow at side and fingers fully extended.
> Place other hand over the head and draw up the hair above and behind the ear.
> Display teeth and gums. Smile![13]

"Social hygiene," the euphemistic term for sexual health, was also encouraged in high schools of the 1920s, spurred in part as a response to the sexual leniency among modern youth and social reform campaigns against venereal diseases. High school biology teachers in New York taught sex education to sex-segregated classes, covering such topics as sexual reproduction in plants, animals, and humans; birth and human development; evolution and eugenics; and leading discussions on the home and family life, morality, and spirituality. Broader social goals were also the objective of organized competitive athletics, which were increasingly seen as a cure-all for delinquency, truancy, and sexual precociousness. In 1918 the New York State legislature enacted a law requiring 20 minutes of physical education a day

the homeroom teacher was also expected to develop a sense of community within the homeroom, to promote a "team spirit" and "cooperative and competitive endeavors."[19] In the properly run homeroom, one writer rhapsodized,

> Life is abundant and most unrestrained, eagerness and joy abound, and success attends all earnest efforts. Here it is easy and "natural" to behave in socially desirable and self-satisfying ways—indeed whatever is self-satisfying is also socially desirable. It is an embryonic community, a purified and idealized democratic society.[20]

Critics of the new reforms in education had quite a lot of fun with such ecstatic phrases. As one contemporary critic of the "poor enriched curriculum" satirized, the new school taught young Americans such necessary skills as

> how to blow his nose and take care of his handkerchief; convert old underwear into rag cats; make and fly kites, dye Easter eggs; cut out sailboats, select dishes in a make believe cafeteria; feed a chipmunk; dance according to approved standards; be interviewed for publication; see beauty in a cake of soap; produce home-made ink; give a school yell; avoid injury by jumping and leaping [and] select beauty queens. . . . What if he cannot read, write, or decipher?[21]

Such biting commentary was based on an unreasonable view of the dominance of social efficiency curricular ideas throughout the curriculum. In actuality, if teachers were expected to take on such tasks, it was *in addition to* teaching students to "read, write, and decipher." Teachers may have been pressured to be creative leaders of social efficiency ideas inside and outside of the classroom, but they were also required to prepare students for what many saw to be the only true objective of their teaching: student proficiency on standardized city and state tests.

TEACHERS AND TESTS

New York City schools presented students with a plethora of tests, including the state Regents Exams for high school seniors; annual achievement tests for all students in composition, arithmetic, spelling, silent reading, and vocabulary; a citywide evaluation of pupil progress and retardation rates; IQ tests; and tests in select schools for the evaluation of the curriculum. Testing was popular among school and government officials alike because it provided taxpayers and government officials with some accountability for student progress in schools. Testing also nicely counterbalanced the demands of an increasingly heterogeneous school population by sorting students by their performance on a standard measurement scale. Whatever the rationale, testing presented teachers with a totally different objective than that of the broad socialized curriculum.[22]

Intelligence testing took American schools by storm in the postwar era, and it was widely praised as the first academic measurement of student ability and potential achievement in school. The Stanford–Binet and Alpha and Beta intelligence tests were originally administered to almost 2 million U.S. Army recruits in World War I as a method of examining and sorting soldiers for specific jobs. Educators immediately saw a correlation with their own work, and by 1925 two-thirds of American cities, including New York, used intelligence tests to classify pupils into homogeneous groups. Intelligence tests helped solve problems of pupil classification by allegedly objective scientific processes, dividing students into comparative strata of ability and career direction. Decisions about tracking were never as scientifically objective as school reformers claimed, however, and intelligence tests became the vehicle for the segregation of students by background, race, and class.[23]

Teachers across the country expressed ambivalence about intelligence tests. Many saw firsthand how the tests themselves were often incomprehensible to foreign-born students and more challenging for a poor urban child with a weak educational background than for a child from a better economic environment. But teachers also had reason to appreciate the IQ test. For one thing, the evaluation of students' supposedly "native" intelligence placed the responsibility for failure on the student, not on the teacher, whose employment record might otherwise reflect such failures. Furthermore, IQ test results were often used as diagnostic tests to track students who were identified as gifted or mentally defective into special classes, leaving teachers with a more homogeneous classroom that was easier to teach than a classroom of students with diverse abilities.[24]

But regardless of the testing results, the actual delivery of IQ tests increased teachers' work. Intelligence tests were designed to be administered by trained experts, but in many schools, teachers were assigned the task of supervising and grading tests. Psychologists criticized this practice, claiming that tests were incorrectly administered by exhausted and untrained teachers, and teachers agreed that the process was both unscientific and time-consuming. To Leonard Covello, then teaching at the overcrowded and ethnically diverse DeWitt Clinton High School in Manhattan, it was nothing less than "intelligence test insanity" when hundreds of students sat at lunchroom tables to take timed tests under the supervision of teachers.[25]

Student achievement tests often served as a method of evaluating teachers' work in the classroom. In some elementary schools, teachers were required to deliver student papers and tests to the principal at the end of the week.[26] One teacher remembered the amount of detailed work required for this task:

> The routine was that on Friday you hand in a set of papers—arithmetic, spelling, penmanship. . . . You had to send it in with a top sheet that said how many students were present, how many were absent, and the average grade in each subject. And the principal would see if the items on the papers that week corresponded to what you were supposed to be doing that week.[27]

At PS 122 in Queens, Alice Marsh's assistant principal was "a bug on spelling" who required teachers to teach, and students to learn the spelling of 10 new words every week. She required weekly spelling tests on the 10 words every Friday, and teachers whose students did not score 100% were criticized. The spelling tests increased teachers' workload as they juggled the demands of the test with their regular instructional responsibilities.

> It was terrible to teach like that. We never had the opportunity to really give the children the spelling that they needed when they'd write a composition. They would mis-spell a word and you wanted to work on that particular word, but you couldn't because you were so busy with the others— the 10 words required by the assistant principal.

To ease their workload and still fulfill the testing requirements, teachers would spell the words correctly for their students, so that in the end, the assistant principal saw only perfect work, whether or not it was the student who wrote it. Teachers ridiculed the assistant principal both for her ideas and because she did not catch the teachers as they undermined her requirements.

> In the bell curve—what you learn about in psychology—there's someone at this end and someone at the other end. And the majority fall in the middle. Now, when you twist that bell curve so that everybody is over on this side, any idiot knows that that's wrong, that there's got to be some kind of manipulation.[28]

Teachers' criticism of testing was based on their definition of an efficient workplace as one that allowed teachers time to complete their assigned tasks properly. City school administrators tended to have a different definition. For example, junior high school teachers in Washington, D.C., objected to the requirement that they grade achievement tests during late December when they were busy with end-of-year reports and preparations for Christmas parties. The school board claimed that there was not enough money to pay for clerical staff to grade the tests and that teachers would learn more about their students by grading their work. But teachers pointed out that they were often assigned to grade the work of other teachers' students, and not their own. In addition, the tests were intended to evaluate the need for extra work for students, yet in only one school had a remedial clinic been established for students who performed poorly on the tests. Indeed, the tests themselves seemed completely wasteful, since they were not based on the city course of study, and only one statistical analysis had been made of the results. Teachers objected not only to the time spent on grading tests during the school year, but also to the seeming uselessness of the tests and to the way in which the tests burdened teachers. The "overfatigued" teacher was less efficient in instruction, they argued, and less able to advise students and support extracurricular activities. In the end, such testing arrangements made both the teacher and the school less efficient.[29]

The same complaint about inefficiency and confusion led New York City teachers to argue that the multiplicity of tests from the state and the city further confused them as they navigated through their already crowded syllabus. Many high school teachers complained that the Regents Exams took up a majority of their time and forced them to abandon creativity in order to teach to the test. Distracted by the demands of tests, teachers had little time or energy to attend to students' other needs.[30]

TIME AND SPACE UNDER SOCIAL EFFICIENCY

Given the confusing emphasis on both broad social education and technical proficiency, it is little wonder that historians have found little evidence of innovative teaching in city schools in the 1920s, even as reformers promoted so many exciting curriculum ideas. In the face of literally tons of documents urging teachers to take field trips, use movies, teach laboratory and library skills, and adopt student presentations, group work, dramatic presentations, and independent projects, historians have concluded that most teachers maintained traditional teacher-centered practices such as rote learning, lecturing, and recitations with the ultimate goal of performing well on the assigned test.[31]

The New York City Board of Education encouraged the development of similarly innovative curricula, although according to teachers, it was far easier to talk curriculum reform than to actually do it. Because curriculum reform ideas were articulated at such a high level—in academic professional associations and school board committees—the supervision and enforcement of real curricular change was minimal. One reason that curriculum reforms did not affect teachers was that teachers and administrators in local schools were simply able to ignore them. With over 600 New York City schools in the 1920s, there was little possibility that the board of education could effectively monitor teacher practice. Nor was it assured that all teachers would be capable of adopting new practices, given their own training and the stressful context of their working conditions. What the board of education encouraged in its teachers' guides was secondary to the demands of the local principal. Teachers recalled some administrators who emphasized not progressive pedagogy but the exact accounting of students' examination grades. Class trips, group projects, and special school assemblies required local administrative approval, and teachers' classroom practice was regularly evaluated by supervisors who might have their own, more traditional ideas about good teaching. Innumerable New York City teachers continued to lead dull, spiritless classrooms throughout the years when curriculum reformers claimed that American classrooms were revolutionized. In the same year that one Brooklyn principal estimated that "an average of one [curriculum] revision a week" was occurring in American classrooms, a nationwide study found that only half of the high school principals surveyed said they had taken steps to reorganize their curriculum and the extent to which that reorganization actually happened was unknown.[32]

Many teachers continued to teach as presumably they had been taught, relying on teacher-dominated lectures and rote methods of learning, and using course material that bore little or no relation to students' lives. Many classrooms of the 1920s resembled the classroom observed in 1912, where the teacher was a "drillmaster" who asked between two and three questions a minute, eliciting one-word or one-phrase responses from students so that students faced an average number of 395 questions a day. Nor did innovative school technologies, supplies, and books necessarily change the traditional classroom experience, because new subjects and new methods could be adapted to conform to old structures and patterns. At PS 45 in the Bronx in the fall of 1920, for example, a teacher led an oral quiz on a film about irrigation in much the same manner that she would have interrogated students after a reading assignment. Students who sat stationary in their desks struggled to remember correct details from the movie in response to the teacher's questions. A 1924 survey of new teachers in city schools found a preponderance of standardized teaching methods and an emphasis on drilling students with questions. One teacher who kept his room of 50 students quiet and orderly had also collected and made new teaching material, and shown much creative promise as a teacher. Yet his district superintendent's support of drilling students threatened to overcome the teacher's potential so that eventually, the observer feared, he would become little better than a "teaching robot."[33]

Even when the board of education supplied supports for teachers, they proved unhelpful. The board published study guides for elementary and secondary teachers in required subjects that presented the aims and objectives of the course, the components of the required syllabus, a bibliography for further research, and suggestions for extra assignments and activities inside and outside the classroom. Required course-of-study guides existed for separate academic subjects and for such elementary school activities as organized recess, sewing and constructive work, and library work. Some course-of-study guides for secondary teachers were upwards of 50 pages long for each individual subject. Given the sheer bulk and variety of course-of-study guides, many teachers found that the mere mechanics of sorting through, reading, and making sense out of the guides interfered with their usefulness.[34]

The reasons that teachers may not have been as creative in the classroom as educators would have liked may have had as much to do with the nature of their working conditions as with their own abilities, temperament, and commitment to students. Many teachers may not have had the time, energy, expertise, or initiative to take on the mass of new expectations demanded of them. Schools did not always provide the recommended supplies and materials, and teachers were not given extra time to take on the extra workload of redesigning their classrooms. Nor did the introduction of extracurricular and social service work in schools lessen the emphasis on academic work or teachers' requirements to complete the standard curriculum and testing required by city school boards. Academic work was still considered the core purpose and regular work of schools and teachers. Indeed, the parallel emphasis on academic testing confirmed just that.[35]

Across the nation, teachers commented frequently about the intensification of their work, describing their complicated schoolday to their teacher associations, unions, and newspaper reporters, and begging for relief. They asked for more order and regularity in their schoolday and more time to actually teach a lesson. In monthly school council meetings in Chicago, teachers complained that their daily schedule was constantly being interrupted by student monitors, collections for penny lunch, moving chairs to and from classrooms for assemblies or gymnastic work, bulletins from the principal to be read to students, the delivery of supplies, pupils passing to the doctor and nurse, inquiries about lost articles, window washers, carpenters, painters, cleaners, visiting administrators, teachers, or pupils, and a range of other inexplicable events. A teacher in one school reported that her classroom was interrupted daily for winding the clock. Responding to the call from their large membership in 1926, the Brooklyn Teachers' Association sent the New York City board of education a resolution against the conducting of fund-raising or membership drives that interrupted teachers' daily classroom work.[36] A junior high school teacher in Memphis wrote a poem about "just another day" at school where teachers struggled simply to find a moment to teach between interruptions by the school nurse and dentist, club announcements, and a visitor carrying a stack of mental tests with instructions to the teacher for grading. All day the teacher tried in vain to begin a lesson, always to be interrupted. In the poem's denouement, the lead story of the next day's newspapers read: "Teacher placed in straight jacket, Beats head upon the floor" as the teacher cried:

Place me on Sunium's marbled steep,
Surround me with the ocean deep;
Put a class within my reach,
And then, good Lord, just let me teach![37]

Researchers confirmed the sources of teachers' frustrations. According to one study, the amount of time that urban high school teachers spent working outside the classroom increased significantly in the early 1920s because of a combination of forces, including an increased emphasis on moral and vocational guidance, the requirement of more accurate and comprehensive accounting reports, and overcrowded schools. Teachers spent less time on teaching than on miscellaneous work in schools, including lesson preparation, conferences with students, department and committee meetings, school, club, and society meetings, clerical work, and the supervision of social activities. One 1926 study of elementary teachers' workloads across the country found that 15% of their time was spent in supervision of recess, study hall, and other nonclassroom events. At least half that amount of time was spent on school-related work before and after the schoolday. A 1917 study of the amount of time that New York City teachers spent on school-related activities after the six-hour schoolday reported that elementary teachers spent 1½ hours a day, and secondary teachers spent 2½ hours a day, for an average total of 55 hours per month spent on unpaid extra activities.[38]

In a period when administrators touted the efficiency of modern school management, much of teachers' extra work was the result of administrative inefficiency. Some new services were promoted in curriculum guides as valuable educational components before they were actually introduced to schools, and teachers were forced to improvise. At a new elementary school in Queens in 1925, the most basic classroom supplies, including chalk, erasers, paper, and books, did not arrive until November. Teachers had to learn how to make do on their own as they waited for basic supplies. One teacher recalled how she improvised:

First of all you made the kids buy their own notebooks. Then you went out and bought the chalk out of your own pocket. And anything else you needed you bought out of your own pocket because you knew you couldn't survive without something there. There was a mimeograph machine in the office and you'd try to steal some time and make some duplicates for the kids. . . . Some teachers were able to sing, but I can't sing. But I'd read them stories.[39]

The school library was promoted in the 1920s by librarians, educators, and children's book publishers as a central location to teach reading and cultural appreciation. The library, ideally envisioned as a separate room with good lighting and a quiet, graceful ambiance, was the perfect place to run reading and discussion groups and to present educational slide shows and map-reading exercises. A Library Extension Division of the New York State Education Department was created in 1925 to supervise, inspect, and advise school libraries and to certify school librarians, but most elementary schools still did not have libraries through the 1930s. The promotion of library activities without the requisite resources in many schools meant that teachers took on extra work to literally build libraries. Teachers at an elementary school in Manhattan designed reading hours for "bad boys" to teach appropriate reading habits and the worthy use of leisure time to potentially delinquent students. But since the school had no formal library room, teachers and students renovated an assembly room, collected bookcases from around the school building, and started a fund drive to buy books. Since there was no school librarian, teachers volunteered their lunch break to supervise the library hour and to monitor students' reading habits, borrowing practices, and discussion groups.[40]

Movies, too, offered an innovative component to the classroom yet in practice created more work for teachers. As an educational medium, movies were particularly popular during the decade when the film industry exploded into popular culture. Some educators looked to adapt the new medium to the school's advantage, an enterprise that delighted the emerging film industry in its search for larger markets. Local and national education journals published regular articles that described and promoted the educational films of various companies. Even the world-famous educator John Dewey promoted the introduction of movies and slides into schools in the 1920s as a welcome visual element to classrooms that could greatly enhance geography and science lessons with pictures of real places and objects. But new and highly touted school supplies such as movies were not always available in schools, and teachers often had to improvise by buying their own supplies. Film equipment was expensive and the New York City Bureau of

Visual Instruction, which provided films for schools, was poorly funded, reaching less than one-sixth of city schools in 1924. Teachers relied on private companies to furnish visual equipment, and the Museum of Natural History distributed an especially popular set of slides to city schoolteachers, as did the New York State Department of Education. Parents and teachers led fund-raising drives for the purchasing of film projectors and the popular hand-held stereopticon slide projector or larger slide projector. For teachers, the expectation that a good classroom be one that utilized new visual aids meant that they were often forced to search for those supplies, thus adding more work to their already crowded school day.[41]

One proposed administrative solution to the increased expectations of the curriculum was to lengthen the schoolday, thereby increasing the technical ability of teachers to complete their extra duties. For example, the city superintendent of Washington, D.C., schools proposed extending the length of the high school day one-half hour so as to allow for extracurricular work. Given the increasing social demands on schools, the superintendent argued, teachers simply could not accomplish the expected clerical work and socialization education in the 10-minute slot allocated to homerooms. But the local teachers union argued that this would actually decrease the efficiency of the schoolday by allowing for the inclusion of even more activities. Furthermore, the union questioned whether the problem of extra assemblies cutting into class periods was necessarily solved by allowing more time in the school schedule. Perhaps the schedule itself could be made more lean by cutting back on the number of assemblies and other extra activities?[42]

New York City teachers faced a similar problem and had posed similar suggestions for improvement. Since the turn of the century, New York City high school teachers' workday had increased from five hours of classroom time to seven with no related wage compensation. At the same time, the number of periods taught and the size of classes increased, so that in the 1920s some teachers taught more than 200 students per week. In schools running on double sessions, the scheduling shattered any lingering sense of order in schools; teachers lost their lunch period and drove themselves to exhaustion as they raced around the building. Because of overcrowding and inadequate facilities, teachers held their classes and met with individual students in strange, makeshift corners of the building. As a consequence, argued the president of the Teachers Union, "everybody seems to be in somebody's way, with a resultant wear and tear upon teachers." In the face of these intensified burdens, he asked "is it any wonder that educational efficiency suffers? . . . What else can teachers do but conserve their energy or break down?"[43]

In fact, years earlier some teachers *had* tried to do something about the extension of hours in the high school. In 1917, when the board of education proposed to lengthen the high school day, the Teachers Union organized a protest. Three of the teachers involved in the protest were subsequently suspended and six were transferred in what teachers referred to as a "punitive transfer." Joseph Jablonower was transferred from DeWitt Clinton High School in mid-Manhattan to New Utrecht High School near the south shore of Brooklyn, a full two-hour commute from his home in the north Bronx. This, teachers learned, was what could happen to those who organized collectively against central administration orders about their work.[44]

CONCLUSION

To curriculum reformers, the problem of the curriculum in the 1920s was how to educate the nation's youth to be economically productive and socially conscious individuals. To teachers, the problem of the curriculum in the 1920s was how to juggle a complicated collection of curriculum directives and demands with too few resources. In the end, it was the daily demands of local school operations, not organized teacher resistance, that undercut the objectives of social efficiency–oriented school reform and made it particularly inefficient. State and city course requirements, tests, and daily scheduling problems entangled the curriculum so that teachers barely had the time to address their own classroom practices. As a teacher advocate complained to a group of school administrators at a National Education Association meeting in 1919, "too much is demanded by the system of the teacher." A teacher had to be nothing less than a "superwoman" to complete all the curriculum expectations. Students and teachers alike were drowning under the multiplicity of demands of the modern curriculum, which included both academic and socialized curricula. What administrators saw as valuable socialization, teachers experienced as chaos.[45]

The socialized curriculum did more than intensify teachers' working hours; it also reinforced the occupational identity of the teacher as an individual with personal responsibilities to the school. The social efficiency component of the curriculum shifted the weight of teachers' responsibility from academic instruction to social behaviors and furthered the emphasis on the social identity of the teacher. The emphasis on social education meant that teachers who objected to the socialized curriculum were in effect rejecting their responsibility as instructors of patriotism, democratic values, economic self-sufficiency, health, morals, and clean social practices. And such teachers might be suspect of having inferior moral and civic characters. For example, a 1921 bill requiring that teachers and students in New York State salute the flag every day was supported by legislators in part as a means of getting those teachers out of the schools "who have no respect for American institutions."[46] Teachers who complained about the intensification of their work or who requested salary increases to compensate for increased work were excoriated for selfishly thinking about themselves rather than their students' needs. Those who criticized standardized tests were accused of unprofessional and lazy behavior by resisting the better judgment of their superiors. The ideal teacher was a volunteer who willingly took on the extra work of health care educator, librarian, social worker, family guide, and civic model. Such a teacher was a paragon of energy and creativity, independently motivated, but still a passive recipient of the wisdom of his or her superiors. Teachers were required not only to teach certain values but literally to embody those values.

~§ 4 §~

Isolation and Stress:
The Physical Workplaces of Teaching

THE INTENSIFICATION OF CITY teachers' work was embodied in their physical working conditions. If the curriculum presented teachers with a confusing job description, school facilities offered teachers the worst possible working environment to perform that job. New York City teachers in the 1920s worked in old school buildings with broken, dangerous, and filthy work spaces, and under frantic and exhausting schedules. The gigantic size of new school buildings increased teachers' experience of isolation from one another, and the new rooms required by the modern socialized curriculum required extra supervision and special scheduling. In addition, the management of school spaces led to sharp disagreements between teachers and administrators, who often disagreed on the definition of an orderly school building.

Like the curriculum, the nature of school facilities both intensified teachers' work and divided them from one another. The organization of school space and facilities touched teachers on a day-to-day visceral level, affecting their physical strength, their personal comfort, and their time. Adapting to physical working conditions consumed much of teachers' workday, exacting both physical and emotional costs as they struggled with makeshift facilities, intense overcrowding, and a mountain of bureaucratic rules about their use of their workspace. The condition of school facilities also literally divided teachers when they were offered no common workplace or a confusing schedule. Teachers' lack of control over their physical working conditions was emblematic of their lack of control over their work as a whole.

In her discussion of contemporary teachers' working conditions, Susan Moore Johnson argues that a workplace is much more than merely a physical setting: "It is also the context that defines how work is divided and done, how it is scheduled, supervised, compensated, and regarded by others." As research in industrial work has long shown, the character of the workplace both determines worker satisfaction and shapes the possible and potential accomplishments at work. In city schools in the 1920s, the nature of working conditions shaped teachers' social relations and determined the nature of their resistance, solidarity, and identity. The pattern of isolation, individualism, and political passivity that historically shaped teachers' work was literally constructed in the physical workplace.[1]

THE SCHOOL BUILDING CRISIS OF THE 1920s

By 1920, New York consisted of five boroughs that defined the political and cultural framework of the city. The island of Manhattan was traditionally the hub of the urban population and commerce. The boroughs of Brooklyn and Queens on neighboring Long Island, the Bronx to the north, and Staten Island to the south were growing rapidly into major residential and economic centers, thanks in part to the expansive web of interborough subway lines created by the newly consolidated city transit system and a network of bridges. The increased accessibility of these areas to the economic centers of Manhattan spurred a shift of middle-class residents outward, leaving whole neighborhoods of Manhattan almost decimated, while parts of Brooklyn, Queens, and the Bronx that were forest or farmland before the war became suburban communities almost overnight. Some parts of the city were pure cement and brick, barren of any greenery, while other sections seemed as rural as the state of Iowa. In 1930, the same year that the final touches were being added to the Empire State Building in midtown Manhattan, there were more than 250 farms registered within the New York City limits. The population varied in density from more than 500 persons per acre in congested Harlem to fewer than 1 resident per acre in more than 60,000 acres in its outlying sections.[2]

The 600 public school buildings were as diverse as the city itself, reflecting the demography of the expansive metropolis. In predominately rural Staten Island, traditional one- and two-room schoolhouses dotted the landscape. But in the rapidly growing suburbs of Brooklyn and Queens, large institutional school buildings stood like lonely giants waiting for houses and stores to grow around them. In the densely packed city blocks of Manhattan, school buildings were wedged between apartment houses. Because Manhattan's north–south avenues were heavily traveled, schools were built on smaller streets running east and west. To draw as much light into the building as possible, architects designed schools in the shape of a U or H, so the wings received east or west lighting from the open area created by the wings. This open area could also double as a playground area. In some inner-city schools, the flat roof was also caged in with fences and used as a recreational space so that city students could play in the safety of an enclosed blacktop.

Some of the earliest school buildings in the city were designed to be distinctive in both size and style. School architects at the turn of the century adopted the architectural style known as Collegiate Gothic, which visually associated city public schools with medieval European universities and conveyed the message that the public school was a "true temple of learning." DeWitt Clinton High School, built in Manhattan in 1906, was a tall five-story red brick building with a peaked roof and magisterial spires that reached to the sky. Its first-floor facade had large, arched windows and its entrance was preceded by broad stairs and an elegant archway. It resembled a palace that literally towered in both height and prestige over a neighborhood filled with warehouses and tenements. The Gothic castlelike structure of PS 165, built at the turn of the century on the Upper West Side, was described by the urban reformer Jacob Reis as a "palace for the people." But such monumental buildings could also intimidate the poor or newly immigrated student. The architect Lewis Mumford, who attended that school as a child and presumably saw more of the interior, called the structure "prisonlike."[3]

By the early 1920s, many of these monumental buildings were among the most notoriously outdated of city school facilities. One-third of all the city's 600 schools were built before 1900, and half of those (100 schools) were built before 1880. In the entire district of Harlem, no new school had been built in 20 years, even though the population had recently doubled. The antiquated conditions of so many of the city's schools elicited a maelstrom of protest from parents and civic reformers who accused the board of education of risking students' and teachers' health, as well as the educational value and economic efficiency of the school system. Throughout the 1920s, investigators publicized the flaws of the New York City school system with harrowing tales of student lessons in dank basements, dark hallways, and auditorium stages. A survey of city schools by a coalition of civic women's clubs in the early 1920s found that over half of the schools investigated were dreary and dilapidated structures that were desperately in need of paint and repair. Mothers of students at a public school in Brooklyn in the late 1920s reported that their children sat on the cellar floor next to the boilers and lavatories because the school was so overcrowded. In his survey of American schools in the 1920s, writer Upton Sinclair wrote that in New York, the wealthiest city in the world, "the children of the poor are herded into dark, unsanitary fire traps, some of them seventy five years of age; and even of these there is an insufficiency!"[4]

Old buildings presented special problems with classroom ventilation, sanitation, and lighting as well. Outhouses in the backyards of New York City schools were common through the 1930s, although indoor toilets were not always an improvement. Many schools had toilets only on one floor, and often only in the damp and airless basement from which foul odors rose up the stairwells and infiltrated classrooms. In old school buildings with small windows, a classroom of 50 students could be hot, congested, and dark, particularly in the winter, when the stale air of the closed classroom furthered the spread of contagious illnesses. Electric lights were not installed in all of New York City's schools until the mid-1920s, and old buildings were the last to receive electricity. In old schools built in a once-open space but now crowded in by buildings, rooms on the first and second floor would have been especially dark. Health reformers condemned the poorly lit classrooms and those lighted by windows on two or three sides of the classroom, resulting in glare and shadows on the blackboard. Such faulty lighting in American schools, they charged, was one reason that 22% of Army recruits for World War I were rejected for defective vision.[5]

Driven by the public outcry for improved school facilities and by the ever-increasing enrollment rates, the New York City Board of Education initiated a school building program of unprecedented size, spending more money on school buildings in the first 5 years of the decade than in the 20 years previously. The board of education created a superintendency of school buildings, which appropriated $284 million for 154 new school buildings and renovations and additions to 111 schools. In one 12-month period alone, 90 new school buildings were opened.[6]

New school buildings of the 1920s were the products of modern engineering capabilities and reorganized financing systems. The development of reinforced concrete gave school architects quicker and cheaper methods of constructing large schools, and the expansion of manufacturing processes allowed for faster delivery and cheaper costs in standard stock features. In the busy New York City school building department in the mid-1920s, several hundred architects and draftsmen were employed to churn out standardized blueprints of dozens of new schools designated for the growing outer boroughs. To accommodate the rapid enrollment increase, these new schools were huge institutional structures, four or five stories tall, holding 50 to 100 classrooms, some with the capacity of housing up to 5,000 students and more than 150 faculty and staff. Under the ambitious new school construction program of the 1920s, architects designed less elaborate school buildings along a monolithic and cubic layout plan reminiscent of contemporary factories. The more simplistic exterior design of school buildings of the 1920s was less expensive, and it also reflected a new image of the public school as the educator of practical working citizens. Like the purpose of the school itself, the school building represented practical social purpose and economic efficiency.[7]

However stark and simple the exterior, schools built in the 1920s housed a great variety of classrooms, administrative offices, and specialty rooms. The broadened scope and purpose of public schooling in the 1920s was embodied in the modern school building, which provided a kind of hidden curriculum of social efficiency reform ideals. The development of specific curricular movements in education—particularly in industrial and technical education, commercial education, domestic and physical sciences, physical education, and the arts—promised to radically change the simply furnished academic classroom. Given the expectation of the school as a social and cultural agent for poor urban youth, new school buildings were intended to provide facilities that poor families could not provide, including books in libraries, games in playgrounds, medical care in nursing rooms, and healthy food in cafeterias. The school would literally become an expanded house: Some high schools boasted miniature apartments for home economics classes, manual training shops, kitchen and dining rooms, health clinics, play yards, and the new "homeroom." In the most bleak and despairing urban districts, the new school was designed to act as "a peoples' club house," standing as a central resource and beacon of culture in the community.[8]

TEACHERS' EXPERIENCE OF THEIR WORKPLACE

Like the written curriculum, the great expectations of the modern school house were not so easy to accomplish. Indeed, the physical conditions inside modern city schools made it particularly difficult for teachers to get their job done, much less take on the extra responsibilities promised by social efficiency reformers. Teachers who worked in older buildings found few of the specialty rooms and equipment that they needed for their modern curriculum, including laboratory facilities for physical or domestic science, equipment for industrial arts or secretarial studies, or open spaces for dramatic exercises, physical education, or group projects. Older schools built for a curriculum based on readers and slateboards provided few of the most basic modern amenities, such as electrical outlets, bulletin boards, and storage places for books, papers, and other teaching aids. Through the late 1930s at a junior high school in Manhattan, classrooms were designated as science rooms because they contained "a rusty cast iron slop sink or . . . running water at the teacher's desk." In one school, the adaptation of the building's flat roof to a physical education playground was ill-fated because the noise of children playing disturbed the classroom below. Furthermore, the roof leaked. Teachers in old schools also complained about broken clocks and drinking fountains, the absence of soundproof walls for music rooms, and the absence of slide projectors and motion picture machines. Old elementary schools were built to accommodate a small teaching staff and, except for one principal's office, there were no administrative or department offices, libraries, or areas for teachers to conduct conferences with parents or hold tutoring sessions with students. Teachers complained that their lunchrooms were too small, dark, and crowded, that cooking equipment was not provided, that no hot water was available to wash dishes, and that lunchrooms were too inaccessible. In many older buildings, teachers had no lunchroom or lounge at all, requiring teachers to eat in their classrooms.[9]

Most of the city's high schools were so overcrowded that they used old elementary school buildings as "annexes" to accommodate their excess populations. In Manhattan, the DeWitt Clinton High School alone had five annexes to house its bulging enrollment of more than 7,000; only one annex was within walking distance of the main building. High school teachers who were assigned to teach modern science, art, home economics, or secretarial studies to adolescents found themselves cramped into classrooms with tiny desks, flimsy foldable walls or curtains between classes, and minimal supplies. Furthermore, the scattered annex buildings divided the teachers within one school. Some principals used an assignment to distant and run-down annex buildings as a kind of punishment for teachers.

The absence of even the most basic facilities and supplies limited the potential creativity of teachers' work and could only have furthered the dreary atmosphere of the daily classroom. An observer in an elementary classroom in New York City in 1930 described old desks that were stained with ink, no wall maps or globe, and only three potted plants and a small aquarium to brighten the room. Tacked on the bulletin board were a few outdated announcements, a children's weight chart, and some health posters. "There was nothing, tho, of immediate and active interest," commented the observer. "I saw no handwork such as clay or plasticene, and I don't recall seeing any drawings or paintings. I felt the teacher lacked inspiration. She was a good teacher but the work, I gathered, was without incentive." Another observer of a fourth-grade classroom found a stifling environment in a room with few decorations or anything "to call forth the slightest creative impulse of the children who were doomed by law to spend the sunniest hours of their lives there."[10]

Teachers also commented on the physical danger and threats to their health that were caused by their physical working conditions. Around the country, city teachers reported chronic illnesses caused by leaky gas furnaces and faulty ventilation systems, and broken bones caused by tripping through dark hallways, basements, and murky stairwells. Even worse than these

physical problems was the intensity of teachers' physical labor in such unhealthy workspaces. Medical inspectors warned that teachers were prema-
turely aged by incessant work in the stale, airless tomb of the modern urban
classroom, a breeding ground for tuberculosis, bronchitis, and consumption,
where teachers spent their days stooped over desks, barely gasping a moment
of fresh air, and hurriedly eating cold meals in a cramped corner of a room.
The overcrowding of schools and teachers' extended work hours sent many
teachers home at the end of the day little better than "half dead," reported
one commentator.[11]

New school buildings solved some of these problems but raised others.
The sheer bulk of the student body in gigantic new schools presented significant problems of crowd management. At one New York City high school
in the 1920s, student monitors were assigned to a "traffic squad" to prevent
students from colliding in the halls as they moved about the big building.
Teachers, too, raced around the building, leading their classes to and from
their assigned places and attending to their multiple duties as yard monitor, cafeteria supervisor, homeroom teacher, and club advisor. New school
buildings might not even have the design perfection that was promised. The
new Julia Richman High School was built in an area of Manhattan so near
an overhead railway that the noise made 15 classrooms unusable.[12]

New facilities designed for the new social efficiency curriculum also
changed the shape and character of teachers' work, increasing the size of
their workplace and adding new responsibilities. In the modern school of
the 1920s, the social efficiency curriculum required certain modern facilities,
including cooking and gymnasium apparatus, stage equipment and scenery,
colored chalk, slides, films, playground facilities, a school library, school
maps, globes, art materials, and science laboratory equipment. Once ob-
tained by schools, the new equipment required new offices, storage spaces,
and specialty rooms such as the gymnasium, health clinic, cafeteria, library,
and rooms for typing, home economics, art, and industrial work. With these
physical additions came additional activities and inevitable problems: Students and teachers filled the hallways traveling between activities; teachers
spent more time ordering, organizing, and attending to an increasing number of supplies; school budgets filled with requests for films to show on new
film projectors, books to fill new libraries, and lab equipment to fill new
science rooms. Facilities and equipment inevitably broke or ran out and had
to be ordered again. As curriculum reformers, professional associations, and
commercial lobbying groups advocated modern facilities and services, teachers became increasing burdened with additional tasks.[13]

No part of the school building changed more in purpose in this period
than the assembly hall or auditorium. Schools had always used the daily
assembly as a forum for inspirational unification of the school, with the

principal leading the Pledge of Allegiance and teachers conducting student performances. In small elementary schools, some teachers would join their classes together to have little assemblies. Teachers worked together, relying on one teacher to play the piano and others to direct the performance or supervise the audience.[14] One elementary teacher remembered these assemblies fondly:

> I liked the assemblies. We had little plays, we made uniforms. We had Christmas plays and dressed the children in crepe paper. We put on some good shows. It was fun and cozy. The teachers were all very friendly and the atmosphere was friendly.[15]

As both elementary and high schools grew in size and the assembly room was replaced by a large auditorium, the communal function of the daily all-school meeting was transferred to individual homeroom classes where teachers met and supervised students in their classrooms at the beginning of the schoolday. In the largest new schools, the auditorium was used for specially orchestrated school performances once or twice a week. It also served as an available room for study hall or classroom work when schools became overcrowded. The emphasis on the school as a social center also positioned the auditorium as a locale for community events. School architects moved the assembly hall from the second or third floor to the first floor to allow easier public access. Auditorium decoration reflected the growing public importance of the space: New high school auditoriums were large, formal theaters with side balconies, sky lighting, ornate arches, and high ceilings. In the DeWitt Clinton auditorium, murals on the walls beside the stage portrayed the opening of the Erie Canal (Governor DeWitt Clinton's most famous project) and an allegorical scene. At Stuyvesant High School, the stage was overarched by ornate carvings, the balconies were supported by Corinthian columns, and the room was lit by skylights. These public assembly halls for 1,000 students were a far cry from the old-fashioned recitation rooms.[16]

The school cafeteria also began to appear in New York City schools as a response to the needs of an increasing number of poor students. At the turn of the century, health reformers in New York began to lobby the board of education to supply lunch for poor students, having found that at least one-third of students in New York City public schools were undernourished. Free lunch programs were instituted in some of the city's poorest schools, and teachers were assigned duty supervising lunch, collecting milk money, and completing the related accounting records. Still, only 80 of the city's more than 500 elementary schools provided lunchrooms in the mid-1920s, and the emphasis on nutritional health was often counteracted by unhealthy physical facilities. Most students and their teachers ate in their classrooms, outside in the schoolyard, or in the basement, where they sat on benches and ate their meal amidst the drafts, odors, and dampness of the cellar.[17]

One administrative nod to teachers' needs was the separate lounge, which began to appear in new school buildings in the early twentieth century. The teachers' lounge may also have been a legacy of the contemporary movement for protective legislation for women workers. Teachers who worked in old schools without lounges were quick to point out the discrepancy between the legally required rest room in industry and the absence of those facilities in schools. The eugenic tenor of the protective legislation movement for women emphasized the health of future mothers, and school architects agreed that women in the "nervous work" of teaching needed a "home-like informal, attractive room" designed with neutral calming colors and accommodated with comfortable chairs, a small kitchenette and lavatory, and curtains to darken the room for resting.[18]

In 1922 the board of education photographer took a posed picture of a teachers' lounge that exemplified the restorative atmosphere of the ideal teachers' lounge. Seven women elementary school teachers sat quietly in a circle in a sunlit, plainly furnished room, all busy at small tasks. Four of the teachers were sewing and three were reading. To the photographer, this was a calm scene of relaxation and diligent work.[19] In reality, elementary school teachers were not likely to use a teachers' lounge for anything but lunch, since they were in charge of an entire classroom all day with no breaks. And due to increasing clerical work and the extra burden of oversized classes in the 1920s, it is more likely that teachers used their rare free moments to correct papers or complete bureaucratic paperwork, not to darn socks. Even the board's image of a cozy lounge was deceptive. In reality, teachers complained that their lounges (if they had any) were often dreary, windowless rooms with an adjoining toilet. In one elementary school, there were two toilets for 47 women teachers and one for 17 men teachers—all located so close to the teachers' lounge that when the door opened, the odor drifted into the larger room. This lounge doubled as the teachers' lunchroom, a "small, bleak, drab room," noted one visitor, which was made all the less appealing by the fact that it was often crowded with teachers lining up to go to the toilet between classes. According to the visitor, this lunchroom was "to say the least, unappetizing."[20]

TEACHERS, ADMINISTRATORS, AND THE POLITICS OF SCHOOL SPACE

Whatever the actual physical conditions that faced teachers at work, the management of those facilities could exacerbate already difficult working conditions. The administration of the physical space of schools meant more than the maintenance of facilities, spiraling out to questions of purchasing supplies, staffing, scheduling, and the daily social and political dynamics of the workplace. Teachers received orders from a distant bureaucrat who regulated their daily schedule, physical movement, and physical comfort. The dynamics of the control of facilities sharply defined the physical conditions and social relations of teachers' workday. The disparity between teachers' and administrators' image of physical order reflected different notions of efficiency in the workplace.

The physical organization of the workplace reinforced occupational divisions among teachers who were separated from one another by building, floor, and classroom, and distanced from one another by scrambled and hectic schedules that offered no common lunch period or free time to meet. Thus distanced from one another, teachers responded to the working conditions of their school buildings in individual interactions with their supervising administrator that often highlighted their different interpretations of efficiency. What teachers saw as simple solutions to irritating problems, administrators saw as a challenge to their authority in a hierarchical system. When teachers asserted their most basic needs about their physical comfort at work, they were essentially challenging both their principal's individual power and the authority of the larger administrative system.

Some teachers worked under principals who were "fussy" about the appearance of school facilities and who required teachers to monitor school upkeep.[21] A biology teacher who worked in the new James Monroe High School found that her attempt to introduce an innovative hands-on curriculum to her classroom conflicted with the principal's interest in the building.

> James Monroe was a brand new high school when I went there. . . . The principal did not like plants or animals or insects . . . so when I brought white rats in cages and plants into his brand new high school I had to get rid of them. So I had to teach from charts, which hurt me.[22]

Teachers' struggle over the maintenance of classroom temperature epitomized the extent of miscommunication between teachers and administrators about working conditions. School administrators were charged with managing an increasingly complex building with multiplied state regulations about health and safety. In an attempt to create a healthy environment in schools, electrical engineers and school health professionals designed scientific systems of controlling classroom temperature. The installation of modern electrical ventilation in many urban school districts promised a centralized method of controlling the ventilation of classrooms, one that would prevent teachers from making independent (and presumably wrong) judgments about the air quality of classrooms. Indeed, the electric fans and steam-heating systems were designed to work only if teachers followed strict guide-lines about keeping windows shut. But if the ventilation system did not work in the first place—and one study in New York City in the 1920s showed that only 2% of classrooms had functioning systems—teachers threw open their windows in attempts to air out stifling classrooms. Both school princi-pals and supervising engineers admonished teachers sharply for this, derid-ing them for claiming some expertise over scientific issues of health and air quality.[23]

The attempt to control teachers' daily movement within the school space was another bone of contention between teachers and administrators. Prin-cipals continually reminded teachers about the proper way of lining up stu-dents for fire drills, recess, and the beginning and end of the schoolday. The control over *both* students and teachers was implicit in these regulations about school space: It was a teacher's fault if a student was caught running through the hallways, if a student was caught in between classes without a pass, or if student desks were found to be messy. In one New York City school, a teacher remembered that student misbehavior could be blamed on the teacher for failing to maintain order.

> In our school there were up and down staircases. It was a "sin" if a child got caught on the wrong staircase. There was a wooden pass that a child had to carry in the hallway. The teacher was responsible if a child got caught on the wrong staircase or in the hall without a pass. How did that child get out of class?[24]

Teachers also consistently complained to administrators that large classes prevented effective teaching of individual pupils. New York City's standardized classrooms of the 1920s were designed for 40 students in ele-mentary school and 35 students in high school. But the average class size in the mid-1920s was larger: In some areas of Brooklyn and the Bronx, some schools averaged class sizes of 50. High school teachers taught five periods a day, five days a week, with many teachers teaching six classes a day with pupil loads of up to 300 students. Given the enrollment pressures on schools, teachers knew that administrators often evaluated teachers by how many students they could handle without friction.[25] But teachers complained that large class size prevented them from giving students individual attention and that urban classrooms presented particularly challenging students. As one Chicago teacher noted, a teacher might be able to do just as good work with 72 as with 36 students if the teacher's job was merely

> to teach alot of puppets who will sit up perfectly straight and are of the same mentality, and will all listen whether they get tired or not. . . . But our children

are not of the same mentality . . . and a teacher must keep her eye on every single person in the room in order to get that child to pay attention.[26]

But teachers complained in vain, facing enrollment increases and a flood of assertions from the educational research community that class size had no effect on the efficiency of teaching. Nicholas Engelhardt, professor at Teachers College and noted author and consultant on school-building management through the 1920s, argued that if old teachers did not proselytize to young teachers about the benefits of small classes, then the newer teaching staffs would not continue to hold to the outmoded faith in small class size. What he clearly failed to appreciate was that teachers' continued faith in small classes was rooted in a common body of knowledge based on experience.[27]

Opposing views of order and control in the school were highlighted in the seemingly most mundane encounters. One Chicago teacher, assigned to a classroom on the top floor of a school building, spoke not only for herself but also for other teachers who were "a wreck" after daily climbing up and down stairs. Teachers and visiting adults were so winded after reaching the top floor that they had to sit down and catch their breath. One teacher allowed an extended eraser fight between students because she "could hardly speak" from exhaustion.[28] At a five-story elementary school in Queens in the 1920s, many older women teachers were assigned to teach on the fifth floor of the building. The school schedule required these teachers to climb these stairs three or four times a day, as described by their colleague, Alice Marsh, in a rhythmic, if exhausting, litany:

> [You went up the stairs] in the morning and down again at noon, and up again at one o'clock, and down again at three o'clock. But if you had assembly that day, you had to come down again. The assembly was on the first floor. The gym was on the first floor. So if you had gym also, it was up and down, up and down.

Some teachers tried to limit the strain by limiting the number of trips to their rooms. But by cutting corners, teachers cut short their productive work time, trading physical relief for job quality. Alice Marsh recalled how many of the older teachers who worked on the top floors of the building saved their strength by limiting their class preparation.

> I know I used to like to get into my room before the kids got there and I'd get the board straightened out and I'd put something on the board for the kids when they got in. And these teachers, they'd have to sit there in the office and do nothing, just gossip. . . . Because they didn't want to go up and down and up and down.

This practice was apparently permitted by the principal, who saw the teachers sitting in the office at the beginning of the day.

The staircase problem in this school was so disturbing to teachers that they devised a system of monitors, whereby each teacher who had a classroom near a staircase would stand at the top of the stairwell in between periods and oversee lines of students walking the stairwells. This would solve the problem of the supervision of students without requiring teachers to follow their students up and down the stairs. Alice Marsh talked with all the teachers in the building, arranged a schedule, wrote up a chart, and approached the principal with the plan. The plan was received in the following way:

> So I walked into [the principal's] office, and she was very polite, she listened to me until I was finished and then she looked at me with her cold blue eyes and she said: "Miss Smith, *I* am the principal of this school and *I* will decide." And she tore up this thing I had worked so carefully on. Well! She might just as well have slapped my face. I was just so shocked that she was so adamant to have her own way, which was not a good way, which was so hard on the teachers.[29]

This teacher presented what she believed to be a simple request to salvage her health by controlling a small piece of her workplace, an attempt that administrators received as nothing less than legal insubordination deserving of firing. After Alice Marsh's interaction with her principal, she began to keep files of every report and evaluation of her, and she eventually joined the Teachers Union in the hopes of someday equalizing the power between teachers and administrators.

SCHEDULING REFORM

No administrative procedure more directly affected teachers than scheduling schemes adopted by school boards to relieve overcrowding in schools. Under part-time scheduling, certain classes or grades would attend school at select times of the day, thus limiting students' hours in school but spreading the enrollment throughout the day. As many as one-third of all New York City students were on part-time or double-session classes in the early 1920s, and in the growing boroughs of Brooklyn and the Bronx, more than two-thirds of the high schools were on part-time schedules. Part-time scheduling was only a temporary administrative device to accommodate as many students as possible. But some curriculum reformers saw the revised schedule as an opportunity to change not only the shape but also the content of the curriculum. Most notorious of these curriculum and scheduling reforms was the Gary Plan, a system of double-session scheduling developed in the Gary, Indiana, school system during the 1910s. Under the Gary Plan, the maximum utilization of school space was achieved by cycling "platoons" of students through a school building that was well equipped with innovative specialty rooms, such as an auditorium, gym, shop, and music room. Students then received a full day of academic and specialty classes while every classroom was occupied. Progressive educators hailed the program as a scheduling solution to overcrowding that also guaranteed the best of modern curriculum ideas, including class work in the visual arts, industrial education, physical education, and cooperative group work. But the introduction of the Gary Plan to New York City schools in the teens was opposed by working-class parents and teachers, who suspected that the scheme was a thinly disguised attempt to pack more students into schools and to funnel working-class children into vocational programs. Nevertheless, well through the 1920s, the philosophy, if not the structure of "platooning," of the "Gary system," or the "dual plan," still existed in many city school districts in the form of part-time schedules with a progressive curricular rationale.[30]

In the mid-1920s, the president of the New York City Teachers Union lambasted the continued practice of platooning in New York schools as an "educational misfit." The idea of circulating students through different experiences in the school building was in and of itself not a bad idea if the program was applied with appropriate support, he argued. But in New York, the state of schools' physical facilities undercut any progressive plan. Platooning intensified the already difficult situation in elementary schools when children were required to

> run up and down three or four flights of stairs several times a day. Because of the lack of clothing facilities, many had to carry their things with them and on rainy days it was just plain hell. To accommodate all the children on their dual plan many had to use out-door gymnasiums or yards. If it rained they just jammed the yards and stairs and the fire hazard was just unthinkable. As one parent put it: Under this Gary system all the children do is march up and down four flights of stairs, waste time in the Auditorium where they are supposed to be studying since there are too many classes there to enable them to do any effective work or else are engaged in the delightful task of carrying their clothing from room to room.[31]

For teachers, platooning was equally as strenuous. In the high schools, multiple sessions cramped teachers' schedules so that they had no free periods to prepare lessons, give special labs, lead field trips, or meet individually with students. One 1922 study of New York City high schools found that teachers at single-session schools spent an average of 30 minutes a day after school consulting with students, while teachers at double-session schools spent on average "9.7 minutes a day" on this work. Even if teachers had the energy to tutor after school, scheduling would not permit it because of the monumental traffic problems that occurred at the end of each session when up to 2,000 students tried to leave one building to be replaced by another 2,000 within a 10- to 20-minute turnaround period.[32] Double sessions also increased the stress of the teacher's job by creating a tense, tightly scheduled day. The constant rotation of classes kept teachers in almost constant motion, as they raced around large school buildings to conduct classes or supervise students, rushing up and down dark stairwells and through long hallways. One principal remembered that she

> grew very thin from dashing from the fourth or fifth floor down there when there was a problem at lunch. When . . . we had to have double sessions . . . that got very hard. I had to run up and down those five flights of stairs.[33]

Teachers described not only the physical strain of scheduling but also the way in which their professional self-esteem was undermined by a schedule that dislocated them from their colleagues and precluded the existence of a home-base classroom or a common meeting time. "Wandering teachers" moved from classroom to classroom throughout the day. One teacher reported using 19 different classrooms a week. Another teacher drew a direct connection between the absence of a teacher's own classroom and teachers' sense of professional identity by noting that "one's room and one's desk are one's home in the world of work." Not having such a home alienated teachers from one another and caused poor morale among the staff. Such mobility had political ramifications as well: Because teachers were required to supervise student activities outside the classroom, they rarely had time to meet with one another—a situation that discouraged the development of teachers' collective identity and the organization of protective associations.[34]

Elementary teachers had the added responsibility of the constant supervision of their homeroom class of 40 or more children whom they led around a building with as many as five stories and 78 classrooms. Complicated schedules heightened the problem of maintaining order. At PS 53 in the Bronx in the early 1920s, the first session of part-time students was scheduled for one and a half hours of classwork, followed by almost two hours of playground period and lunch, after which teachers had to slow students back down to classwork again. A later group or "platoon" of students and teachers arrived at 9:30 and immediately went to a playground period. Not until 10:15 did this group first settle down into the classroom for an hour and 45 minutes, after which students left class for lunch and an auditorium period in which teachers supervised a number of classes together. Finally, teachers faced a weary class for an hour and 45 minutes at the end of the day.[35]

The supervision of such a schedule was a breeding ground for conflict between administrators and teachers. A retired elementary teacher described the dynamics of her school that ran on the platoon plan in the 1920s:

> The first class [started] at 8:10; the later session began at 9:10 and the first person took her class to the auditorium until the other person came in. . . . I had an assistant principal who was not too bright. He would say: why are you waiting outside that room? I'd say: that class hasn't finished yet. And he'd say: there's an empty in 409. And I would hesitate to go up there with a class of 2nd or 3rd graders because often there wasn't an empty room up there at all and you had to go all that way with your class.[36]

The key to the platoon system was the reliance on the use of specialty rooms to be used by certain classes while other classrooms were used by another platoon of students. In platoon school literature, the time spent in these specialty rooms was intended to broaden the curriculum by providing students with a variety of innovative group activities. Curriculum reformers promoted the auditorium period as a time for spelling bees, artistic performances, talks on manners or morals, music, or student presentations. But in desperately overcrowded schools, the auditorium could become literally a catchall location for classes that were temporarily displaced from their classroom. Teachers found that the emphasis was more often on precise scheduling of students than on actual programming, leading to antagonism between administrators in charge of scheduling and teachers. The same elementary school teacher remembered:

> Then they would put us in the auditorium—the whole grade, maybe six or seven classes and they would tell us to use the time. . . . Once we used slides and the teacher complained that there were no names on the slide and she couldn't tell whether it was a wolf or a fox. And the Assistant Principal said: "what difference does it make?" Things like this would hurt you because you were standing there trying to teach the children and all they wanted to do was to keep the children in their seat.[37]

A Chicago teacher in the same period described the often absurd confusion that part-time systems created and the misguided emphasis on supplies over the lives of students or interests of teachers:

I am in a double shift school and [the administrators] came in and complained because there were two teachers' desks in a room, and at the same time they are not thinking of these children in the corridor or the auditorium. They are particular about the little things. They reported to Mr. McAndrew [the city superintendent] and to my own superintendent because I had an empty desk there that was not being used, and they complained about me, sent three letters, one to Mr. McAndrew, one to Mr. Hitch, and one to my own principal at the same time.[38]

Both elementary and high school teachers found that their workday was defined by the organization of strained school facilities. The persistent problem of overcrowding thwarted many of the good intentions of school reformers when the implementation of complicated scheduling schemes reduced the use of the school building to its most basic function of providing seats for students.

THE ACCIDENT OF GOOD WORKING CONDITIONS

Some teachers found good working conditions almost by accident. Teachers who worked in small old schools that were still in use in the 1920s found that their small size and makeshift character contributed to a positive community climate. Some of these teachers struck a bargain between the disadvantages of outdated facilities and the benefit of small size. When Margaret Jamer started teaching biology at New Utrecht High School in Brooklyn in 1926, she was assigned to teach in an old wooden schoolhouse that served as one of four annexes used to accommodate the overflow of enrollment from the main building. She enjoyed the experience especially because teachers socialized together, creating a warm and pleasant working environment.[39] At Rose Stern's first teaching job in the late 1920s at an annex of Eastern District High School in Brooklyn,

there were about 700 or 800 kids there—all girls. You didn't have the crowds you had at a big school, and you knew everybody in the building. It was really very nice. I was friends with the other teachers.[40]

The collegial relationships that could develop in small schools helped teachers accommodate to otherwise inadequate school facilities. In Rose Stern's annex building, a former large recitation room had been divided into classrooms with temporary walls, creating four classrooms with no linking corridors. Teachers and students had to walk through the front classroom to get to a back classroom. When Rose taught high school secretarial studies

❧ 5 ❧

Administration and Alienation: Teachers' Work Culture Under Supervision

IN A 1928 EDUCATION JOURNAL, a cartoon drawing of "The Super-Vision Demanded in Supervision" portrayed the scope of the work of the ideal school administrator. As the supervisor of teachers, the administrator was expected to maintain the viewpoint of all the interests in the school; to keep up-to-date on pedagogical innovations, social and health needs, and educational psychology; and to keep a reasoned opinion of up-and-coming educational trends. In addition, the supervisor had to maintain "intimate knowledge of each one of her 1000 and 1 teachers" and to foster their scholarship, intellect, character, health, and personality. Such was the grandiose vision of the new supervisor, who would in effect draw together all the strings of the expanding curriculum and social responsibilities of the school of the 1920s. By coordinating all the diversified activities of the modern school, the supervisor monitored and regulated the work of the teacher. Since the administrator was one who "sees all and knows all" in the school, that official would also be the one who controlled all, including the work of the teacher.[1]

The monitoring of teachers' work was a major concern of school reformers in the 1920s. The supervision of teachers had always been important—in the nineteenth century, rural teachers were evaluated on everything from their classroom performance to their social behavior. But in the postwar era, the emphasis on accountability and cost efficiency in schools raised the problem of teacher evaluation to a critical level. Researchers in educational administration developed new methods of evaluating the intricate details of teachers' work. On paper at least, school administrators laid out a highly systematic blueprint of teachers' daily job expectations and a bureaucratic system of supervision and evaluation.

Some historians have argued that as administrative methods of teacher evaluation increased during the early twentieth century, the occupation of teaching was "deskilled" in the same way that industrial workers lost their skills to the highly synchronized assembly line. Expanded school administrations, like the expanding middle management of industry, are said to have created an umbrella of regimentation and bureaucratic work rules that defined teachers' daily tasks so that schools took on the organizational character of the lockstep assembly line of the modern factory. Drawing on Harry Braverman's studies of the deskilling of industrial work in the early twentieth century, these historians have argued that teachers, like their peers in the modern factory and office, underwent a process of systematic deskilling, including a loss of autonomy, an increase of supervision, an emphasis on production and efficiency, and the fragmentation and mechanization of work. Under newly introduced standardized curriculum schemes, tests, and specific job descriptions, teachers are said to have experienced decreased autonomy in their own classrooms, additional routinized tasks, and increased managerial control over each step of the labor process. Teachers' work, like that of the worker in the modern assembly line or secretarial pool, was fragmented and its creative aspects squashed under a powerful system of ordered standardization. Deskilled teachers, according to this argument, would be teachers whose every action in the classroom, and every choice and activity in the school building, would be predetermined, monitored, and evaluated by supervisors.[2]

But teachers' experience of curricula and physical facilities was certainly not characterized by order and rationality. Nor, in fact, were teachers actually "deskilled" by new forms of administrative supervision in the 1920s. Indeed, it is not certain that increased administrative supervision of teachers actually happened in any systematic way in the first place. Certainly many teachers were subject to authoritarian work rules, but often these were piecemeal regulations that required one picayune task in the midst of chaos. According to many teachers, their principals and other supervising administrators were often far from sight and oblivious or ignorant of teachers' work, in part because of the increasing bureaucratic demands on their own time. Furthermore, the intensification of the schoolday undercut many goals for efficient standardization, as the expansive academic curriculum and bureaucratic responsibilities heightened the tension and disorder of the workday. Oftentimes, the increasing complications of the modern school actually increased teachers' ability to control parts of their own labor. In the intensely tangled school building, teachers were often able to surreptitiously undercut or sidestep administrative regulations.[3]

Because of the weak and inconsistent implementation of supervisory procedures, teachers were sometimes allowed to continue their regular work in the classroom, neither hindered nor helped by supervisory administrators. As it was, teachers learned how to take on the most challenging part of their

job through an informal work culture of informal advice and support systems within the school building. Far from being deskilled, many New York
City teachers felt that they developed additional skills of improvisation and
accommodation as they struggled to learn how to teach. Through informal
underground networks, teachers were able to undermine or short-circuit the
effect of supervision by taking advantage of administrators' own ambivalence about supervision. Teachers' responses to supervision thus illustrate
powerful moments of teachers' collective work traditions in an otherwise
oppressive and alienating work climate.

THE SCIENTIFIC RATING OF TEACHERS' WORK

Most of the administrative reforms introduced to schools in the 1920s were
guided by principles of scientific management, a theory of labor management relations developed in early-twentieth-century industry to address the
problem of workers' inefficient production. Scientific management was often
dubbed "Taylorism" after its founder and chief promoter, engineer Frederick
Winslow Taylor, who identified the problem of the industrial workplace as
one of unclarity and imprecision in workers' defined job tasks. According to
Taylor, if managers did not understand the exact components of their workers' assigned tasks, they could not fully control them. Taylor's solution to
this problem was the identification of each task to be performed by workers,
the careful description of the order and process of completing the task, and
precise methods of supervision and evaluation of the completed work. Such
scientific methods of charting out workers' job tasks were intended to give
the supervising managers control over all the components of the workplace.[4]

Scientific management theory in the school followed the same principles
as on the factory shopfloor: the clear defining of individual teachers' tasks
so that managers could better monitor and evaluate those tasks and account
for financial expenditures throughout the school system. In his famous study
of scientific management in schools, Raymond Callahan referred to early-
twentieth-century educators' new obsession with cost accounting as a "cult
of efficiency" in which the budget, not student learning, became the priority
of the school organization, in which schools emphasized accounting procedures over learning processes, and in which school administrators were mod-
eled on business managers, not intellectual leaders.[5]

The analogy between schools and business was a common one in educational reform literature of the 1920s. In the decade marked by President
Calvin Coolidge's dictum that "the chief business of the American people is
business," school administrators continually praised the corporate models of
management in use in the notoriously profitable American business enterprises. Reformers unabashedly adopted factory metaphors of scientific man-

agement to their curriculum work, referring to students as "raw material," the school as the production "plant," and the ideal curriculum as a plan calculated under "conditions of maximum theoretical efficiency." A New York City district superintendent made a direct connection between rating teachers and workers: Both needed experts to identify the most valuable tasks to complete and then to supervise their accomplishment, both were assigned work that could be objectively evaluated, both earned benefits if they completed them correctly and were eliminated if they did not, and both would improve the efficiency of their institution if they completed their tasks correctly. Conjuring up images of industrial efficiency, a high school principal in Oakland, California, described the school that efficiently supervised teachers as one that was "a factory flooded with light and teeming with activity under the skilled hand of the electrical engineer." "Teaching is a business," the president of the Chicago School Board brashly told his city's principals at the beginning of the 1927 school year. "You are salesmen. Your commodity is education. You must satisfy your customers, the taxpayers."[6]

According to this new management theory, schools could only be accountable to the public if teachers were held accountable to schools. To educational administrators inspired by the theory of scientific management, teachers' classroom work was the most unscientific quarter of the entire school organization. One reason for this was that teachers seemed intent on maintaining their right to independent judgment in their work—a practice that undermined any attempt to create a standardized system of education. Teachers were in effect defying work rules by relying on their own experience and remaining ignorant of the new research on effective pedagogy, classroom organization, intelligence studies, and other findings from new centers of educational research. It was teachers' individual judgments, their "rule-of-thumb estimate" of their students that produced the most waste in education, according to the superintendent of New York City schools in the mid-1920s. Teachers needed to be guided toward the most modern practices in schools, and then closely monitored.[7]

New rating schemes were developed that clearly identified teachers' tasks and allowed for the evaluation of their performance in much the way that Taylor had devised for factory workers. In New York City a semiannual rating of teachers was required for teachers' renewal of licenses and promotion. The rating form itself was a single document with categories of teacher performance and measures of evaluation that the principal completed and forwarded to the central office. Until 1922, New York City teachers were rated in eight categories: instruction, discipline, teaching ability, scholarship, effort, personality, control of class, and self-control. These categories were evaluated by grades, A through D. The system was uniformly disliked by teachers, who generally approved of simple rating forms with fewer categories and the evaluations of satisfactory and unsatisfactory. The grading sys-

tem, teachers argued, allowed too much subjective judgment on the part of
the evaluator to the extent that the grades were meaningless. The board of
education eventually agreed, in part, and the new rating system introduced
in 1922 evaluated a teacher as satisfactory or unsatisfactory—but for five
chief categories with 26 subdivisions, including the teacher's "personal tidi-
ness," grammar and use of the English language, ability to cooperate with
other teachers, and skills in questioning, drill, classroom management, and
"power to interest."[8]

Modern technology, too, contributed to the systematic overseeing of
teachers' work. Employee time clocks were introduced to some New York
City schools in the 1920s. Teachers were required to be in their classroom
at least 20 minutes before the opening morning session; those who arrived
late lost part of their daily wage, and the error was noted in their annual
rating. The use of public address systems promised to be the most effective
monitoring device of all, since it gave principals the opportunity to "observe,
with both ear and eye, what is going on in any given classroom, without
either teacher or pupils being aware that their acts are being noted." A promotional article for a school public address system in 1928 visually repre-
sents one administrative vision of the ideal position of teachers in the school
building. In the illustrative cartoon, an oversized woman principal stands at
a lectern speaking into her microphone. At her feet is a cut-out of multiple
classrooms of miniature teachers and students, the students all sitting in
rows, the teachers all standing at the front of the classroom with identical
pointers raised. Each class is blocked off from one another by walls; they are
self-enclosed spaces, open only to the giant principal whose all-seeing eyes—
and now voice—transmit information to them. The public address system,
notes the advertisers, "brings the largest school together as if all classrooms
are one." And, indeed, the school does become one—all under the principal's supervision.[9]

THE PROBLEM OF CLASSROOM SUPERVISION

The supervision of teachers' work in the classroom was the most traditional
method of evaluation. Local administrators were expected to visit their
teachers regularly to evaluate their classroom practice. But educational reformers had recently begun promoting a new notion of supervision that emphasized pedagogical guidance and support. The newly conceived supervisor
was supposed to know intimately the course of study, to understand the
aims, objectives, and underlying principles of each subject and the standards
required in each subject. Supervisors were supposed to be up to date on
current curricular and pedagogical innovations and to maintain a consis-

tently sensitive, supportive, and advisory role with all of the teachers under their charge. No longer were principals expected to be merely administrative "directors of routine," but leaders of the entire school, providing nothing less than "educational engineering and generalship."[10]

Teachers tended to approve of this portrait of the advising school administrator. Principals had a great deal of autonomy in New York City schools, and teachers relied on them to conduct the administrative affairs of the school efficiently enough so that the daily academic business of teaching could get done. If the principal's version of academic business involved close supervision, extra monitoring of teachers' classroom work, and testing of student performances, teachers did not necessarily object, especially if the principal was competent and respectful of the teacher's classroom goals. In fact, many teachers longed for competent and sympathetic supervisors to offer advice about specific classroom problems. How to ensure that students understood the assignment? How to lead an exciting class discussion without losing control? What to do with the student who insisted on chewing gum behind the teacher's back? City teachers described effective supervisors as those who led demonstration lessons, held conferences after a classroom observation, and offered practical suggestions for discipline problems. Teachers appreciated supervisors who offered encouragement, inspiration, and good humor and who provided specific guidelines and practical suggestions. Such a supervisor provided what urban teachers most needed: an efficient, supportive administrator who tried to lighten the burden of the classroom.[11]

But such thoroughness was a tall order for urban school administrators, who, like teachers, saw their jobs expanding in scope and function in the 1920s. District superintendents faced an avalanche of administrative responsibilities, and bureaucratic delays were so commonplace that one observer described the city school system as one that ran "by inertia rather than by intelligent forceful decision." Twenty-seven district superintendents were assigned to supervise 30,000 teachers in more than 600 city schools. They scrambled to visit as many teachers as they could at least once a year for at least part of a class period. One district superintendent supervised 1,000 teachers in 21 schools, making classroom visits that averaged barely 20 minutes. It was especially critical to supervise new teachers for probationary approval, but in the early 1920s, when an average of 1,500 new teachers a year entered the school system, district superintendents faced 75 to 200 new teachers a year. Some district superintendents estimated that they gave less than 5% of their time to teacher supervision, and those visited were primarily teachers with significant enough problems that a complaint had been made of them.[12]

For principals, too, the demands of supervision weighed on their already crowded time. The school principal was in charge of an increasingly complex school operation, including building management, student academic and behavioral issues, and employees. Principals acted as business manager and community and professional leader while keeping up with such daily administrative tasks as ordering and distributing supplies, maintaining school records, and responding to regular and unusual responsibilities emanating from the district and central city office. In schools with enrollments of 2,000 to 3,000 students, often scheduled on double sessions, the job was particularly demanding. A principal who tried to live up to even the minimum of these expectations and job requirements would still have little time for teachers.[13]

Given administrators' other priorities, teachers often found themselves stranded in their classrooms with little or no reliable support. Some teachers described supervising administrators who were inept or hardly even attentive to teachers' needs and who were demanding and authoritarian. One teacher described the school in which he taught as a good place "if one has no questions to ask concerning method, content and so on, and enjoys being left entirely on his own." Chronicling his own disappointments, the teacher noted lost opportunities for the principal to encourage and advise him in his first year teaching. During his first supervisory experience, the principal made no verbal or eye contact but "kept a stony stare straight ahead" until he left, after only 10 minutes. Teachers were confused by supervisors like this one who gave no feedback about a lesson and who left teachers wondering how their performance had been graded.[14]

Perhaps as common as the oblivious supervisor was the administrator who paid too close attention to teachers' every move. These were the notorious principals who seemed intent on controlling teachers' every step through personal authority. This was an old-fashioned and notably unsystematic form of leadership, based on the personal power of intimidation, not on the structured rules of an organizational system. The principal of one elementary school in 1930 was described by a visitor as one who led by the force of her own "self-centered personality." She was like a distant autocrat, not someone who nurtured teachers. Instead, she directed teachers to abide by her wishes and follow the prescribed curriculum. As long as teachers did not cross this principal's path, they were rewarded with a kind of freedom in the classroom.[15]

In other schools, teachers suffered more idiosyncratic leadership. They bristled under supervisors' poor timing, insensitive comments, lack of judgment or understanding of the classroom, and unjust ratings.[16] "You feel a depression in the air from the moment you begin to teach in some schools," explained a New York City teacher to a reporter early in 1922:

It's as though some one at the top were pushing down hard and the rest kept pushing until it reached you. Suddenly from out of the blue the principal or assistant swoops upon you almost breathless and asks for a lot of detail that you didn't think was expected. You catch the panicky feeling and rush around madly, letting the teaching slide.[17]

Another teacher remembered that her principal and his assistant created an aura of aloof authority.

Once in a while they would walk up and down the school, they'd open the door and look in and keep going. They never came in to look at the lesson and analyze it or call you in to talk about it. They would come down to the yard—2,100 kids there were, all lined up and you couldn't hear a sound.[18]

Another teacher remembered "the feeling of dread" when the door opened because she feared a particularly cruel supervisor.[19] This kind of supervisor, noted one teacher, "whose mission should be one of light, casts instead a cloud over the teaching staff."[20]

TEACHERS' WORK CULTURE UNDER SUPERVISION

Given the confusion of the workday and the absence of support, teaching was lonely work. Surrounded by children, and sharing close spaces with other adults, teachers were still strangely disconnected from one another as they taught in their classrooms, monitored the hallways and yards, and went home—"a lone creature in the wilderness of indifference," recalled former teacher Angelo Patri. But woven into the hectic and isolating workday were informal communication links, traditions, and networks that connected teachers and helped them to combat the hardest parts of their work, including the alienation and insecurity caused by the inconsistent supervisory practices. From jokes about supervisors to supportive information networks, city teachers helped each other through what they all understood to be the most stressful part of the job. Teachers' work culture thus provided the means to critique the authority of supervisors whose methods they disliked and to articulate their own definitions of good teaching.[21]

New teachers were in particular need of support because they often found that their experience in training school had not prepared them for the problems of a real classroom. One teacher remembered that "all the background in school on how to teach had not prepared me to actually face a class of forty children." New teachers' first experiences in school were like an initiation rite to the occupation whereby they learned early on that they had to make it on their own—a necessary lesson if they were to survive in an occupation in which overworked teachers rarely had time to help one another and in which supervisors and evaluators were often inexperienced, unhelpful about classroom practice, or not even available for comment. However painful the process, new teachers were quickly weaned away from any expectation of support and guidance and taught to survive on their own—thereby taking on the major attributes of their colleagues' work culture. New teachers were thus encouraged by their colleagues to teach themselves how to teach and to pick up tips from any available source. Some new teachers found friendly colleagues who taught them how to negotiate the particular politics of the school building but stopped at giving actual advice about teaching. One teacher remembered that as a new teacher, nobody helped her. "A teacher or two might have made a few suggestions. And if I had a question or two I knew I could ask people." [22] Another teacher remembered a colleague who

> was very helpful, not in actually showing me how to teach but in my relations with other teachers. If there was something I didn't understand about how the school worked, I could ask her. It was easy to talk with her; I felt free. . . . She helped me in my relationships with the other persons in the building. [23]

In high schools, some teachers found help from other teachers in their own department, as high school teachers tended to bond more closely around their subject areas. A science teacher remembered that it was a fellow teacher, not a supervisor or department chair, who introduced her to the intricacies of the job and offered herself as a teaching model.

> She took me under her wing and showed me things in the laboratory and let me come into her room and let me watch how she taught. My department head didn't help at all. [24]

Such interactions could be very fruitful as teachers learned from one another's immediate classroom experience. One teacher remembered that because her high school department head ignored his staff, the young teachers joined together and provided support and informal supervision for one another. "So almost by accident [the department head] had a group of very bright, alert teachers who had taught each other." [25]

When the isolated classroom was disturbed by an intimidating supervisor, teachers tried to diffuse the anxiety by drawing on the collective sympathies of their colleagues. Sometimes this was literal support when teachers coordinated information networks with whispers or a prearranged code to warn unsuspecting teachers about an unannounced supervisory visit.[26] Help could also come from surprising places: a student in Dorothy Meyer's class had severe reading problems, and she was working with him after class to improve. Yet for all the hours that she gave him, the boy could never read. One day the superintendent came to the class:

> And he calls on John to read. And John reads! I was so nervous that I was walking around the classroom and I saw that John was holding the book upside down. He had a very good memory and we had just worked on that story. The superintendent never knew the difference.[27]

The experience of supervision became a kind of rite of passage that bonded teachers. In a poem intended to console her colleagues, a teacher at PS 4 in Queens penned her thoughts about the rating and supervision system in her local teachers' journal in 1923:

> Oh, they mark us in the springtime,
> And they mark us in the fall,
> And when the game is new to us
> They mark us most of all.
> The Superintendent leads them all,
> The King Pin marker he;
> The very path he treads is marked,—
> by many a quaking knee.[28]

Teachers undercut the authority of disliked supervisors by portraying them as stupid or lazy or by writing them off as old-fashioned, boring, or eccentric. Gender and ethnic stereotypes were often used to bolster teacher criticism: Younger women teachers might discredit a female supervisor for peculiar fashions ("she wore high-necked collars and long sweeping skirts"; "she used to wear high heels and dyed hair"), and they would satirize authoritarian male supervisors by overemphasizing their size, their "great big voice," or their presence as "king pin."[29] A female Jewish teacher remembered her male Irish principal with all the common stereotypes of the day.

> He was about ten feet tall. He was a very bright man but he always had a bottle of liquor in his drawer. He was always in very good spirits: a big bulky fellow, an Irishman.[30]

Teachers also defended themselves by asserting that administrators knew nothing about the gritty realities of the classroom. Familiar as they were with the daily behavior of children, teachers were the first to recognize that the regular patterns of the schoolday did not always fit with the expected program of a supervisor. Years later, retired teachers enjoyed remembering when administrators hurriedly left the class room when delicate subjects such as sex were raised in class discussion. Elementary teachers, in particular, sometimes found that administrators felt out of place with the rhythm of a classroom of small children. Asserting the validity of their own expertise, teachers took pride in recognizing that students learned from their teaching technique even if the supervisor disapproved:

> One time there was a fire across the street. My students had never seen fire engines before so I said: go look out the window. The principal chose that time to come in and she ordered them back to their seats. She looked at me as if to say: what are we putting in the classroom! She didn't see what I saw as a young teacher: that the kids would learn something by looking out the window.[31]

A comedy written and produced at a community center by a Teachers Union member mocked both the overly regulatory character of school management and the administrator's lack of understanding of daily school life. In the play, a superintendent accused a young teacher of excusing a student from her class without permission "to proceed on an unknown errand to an unspecified destination requiring an indeterminate length of time to perform, at the request of a person or persons whose identity must remain shrouded in secrecy." The superintendent suspected that the student was sent to deliver a message to nearby strikers, and he threatened to fire the teacher and expel the student. But in the denouement, the mysterious errand was revealed to be nothing more than a request for delivery of chicken salad for a classroom lunch party, and the audience cheered at the stupidity of the pompous administrator. In this way and in countless interchanges in the hall and teachers' lounge, teachers could neutralize the tension of supervision by satirizing the procedure as nothing more valuable than "snoopervision by stupidintendents."[32]

PLANNING FOR THE PLAN BOOK

Teachers were also evaluated through a daily plan book in which they charted out their lessons for each teaching week. This, too, was a monitoring scheme that promised to deskill teachers but that in practice became little more than a tiresome obstacle for teachers to circumvent. Plan books were generally required for elementary teachers and were evaluated by the school principal or assistant principal. High school teachers did not always have a plan book, but they did have to follow the syllabus, and some departments required teachers to submit their weekly plans for the department chair to evaluate. Regardless of the differences among schools, the goal of the plan book was to organize teachers' work in a written format and submit it to a supervising authority for review.[33]

Many teachers saw the value of writing a prescribed lesson plan that structured the day in the classroom. The plan book could work as a roadmap for organizing class activities, although the best plan was also flexible, allowing teachers room to rearrange their day according to particular classroom needs.

> It was easy to make up the plans. I was told I had so many minutes per week and I had to distribute those minutes with so many set subjects. I could make up my own schedule for the day except I was given certain times when I'd go out for play time or auditorium. . . . It was easier to work when it was structured.[34]

But like so many other parts of teachers' work, the chaotic nature of the school itself could undermine the order that was promised by the plan book. Angelo Patri remembered that after he had arranged his lesson to follow the five formal steps of instruction laid out in his curriculum guide, students immediately disrupted that order, initially leading him to blame himself for designing a faulty plan.

> Almost before I could make the first point of the lesson some child was bound to shout out the conclusion that should, according to my understanding of authority, have come at the end of the teaching process. This left me high and dry. The children refused to think according to the plan.[35]

The value of the plan book was also affected by the way in which the supervising administrator used it. Some teachers believed that their supervisor used the plan book merely to monitor their classroom activities. Other teachers whose administrators rarely even looked at their plan books felt that the entire procedure was another example of needless paperwork that distracted them from actual teaching. Teachers who worked under principals who strictly required the plan book felt that the method severely limited their creativity in the classroom.

> We had to make a plan for the whole week. . . . Monday from 9 to whatever, 10 to whatever . . . and they left almost no room for change if the teacher herself thought it was a better thing. If, for example, the stu-

dents didn't understand the material and you wanted to repeat it the next day, you couldn't because you had to follow the plan book.[36]

An anonymous teacher's poem in the English teachers' professional journal captured the longing of some teachers to break away from the planned lesson to catch students' interest in a more personable and creative way. Entitled "A Rebel Song," the poem illustrated the tension inherent in the teacher who sought to complete her assigned task in "the well-wrought lesson plan," while longing to design her own method of teaching that she believed would be more effective:

> The straight and ever narrow way,
> Paved with a well-wrought lesson plan,
> Points to a brilliant future day,
> When methods win and aims succeed.
> But oh! the joy to break our bonds
> And ramble in some winding path,
> Where eager youth at last responds
> And shy hopes brave a softened light.[37]

Teachers found a variety of ways to undercut the restrictions of the plan book. At schools where supervisors were inattentive to plan books, teachers did "bluff work" by copying last year's plan book into the current year's, or describing the previous week's lesson instead of planning for the forthcoming week. Teachers were not supposed to work on their plan book during class time, which presented a real burden for elementary teachers, who had no free period during the day. Some teachers designed quiet study lessons for students, leaving them time to complete the plan book.[38] One teacher found that by deviating slightly from the expected purpose of the plan book, she could document successful lessons to use for subsequent years.

> You were supposed to write in the plan book what you were going to do. But I'd write in good lessons that I just did because maybe it's something you can repeat. In the classroom, even if you plan the work, it doesn't always work out as you plan. Things come up and things develop and it's an entirely new lesson than you had planned. I'd say: Gee, that turned out so good, it's going in the plan book.[39]

Early on in their careers most teachers learned what their supervisor demanded of the plan book and completed it accordingly. This subversion of one intention of the plan book—to monitor teachers' classroom behavior—was furthered by school administrators who did not always check the plan book at the end of the week as they were supposed to. Teachers learned from one another which supervisors did or did not read plan books.

You learned from another teacher what to put in the plan book. Nobody really told you. I don't remember getting any really good comments from my supervisor. . . . I don't remember any point being made of the plan book in our school. We had to have them but there was never anything made of them. We learned all that from the other people.[40]

One high school teacher found a novel way to circumvent the restriction on her activities as well. As her colleague remembered:

There was this girl who taught in the English Department. Let's say Thursday first period she expected the Chairman to come to observe her. She said: "I have two plans. One for if the Chairman comes, one if she doesn't."[41]

Teachers also learned how to circumvent other classroom requirements set up by local administrators. Teachers were required to teach penmanship by the Palmer method, which required the teacher to provide students with a precise model of perfect handwriting, often displayed on the wall or over the blackboard. In St. Paul, Minnesota, for example, teachers were required to send their principal weekly assignments of their own penmanship, which were returned with criticism and comments. Some New York City teachers who had imperfect handwriting asked friends to write the model handwriting for them. When another teacher learned that her superintendent required students to have perfect handwriting, she cut out printed examples of Palmer handwriting samples and posted them in her room to make it appear that her students had done the work.[42]

With both the plan book and the penmanship requirements, teachers learned what supervisors wanted and performed accordingly. One visitor to New York schools in the mid-1920s noted that the "working rule" among teachers was to "find out what supervisors wanted, be prepared to give it to them when they call, then forget about it until the next visit."

For instance, one inspector's ideal was "pep," as expressed by quick movements, shouting and loud voices on the part of both teachers and children. All the teachers in this district were energetic, snapping their fingers at the children and urging them to run to the board, speak louder, etc.[43]

This behavior should not have surprised anybody, and in fact it made perfect sense to one district superintendent of schools who understood that the teacher was accommodating to the principal in the same way the principal accommodated to the superintendent. As Howard K. Beale wrote in his study of political restrictions on American teachers, "discipline, or even the threat of discipline is unnecessary when teachers generally realize that non-conformity injures them and that conventional ideas and implicit obedience are the means to professional advancement." This dynamic was furthered when the teachers were women and the administrators were men "who often learn how to bully the women under them." A few brave souls dared to live their own lives in schools, Beale noted, but "most teachers soon learn that it is far pleasanter and more profitable to conform."[44] But as many teachers attested in their tactics of subverting supervisory practices, conformity was sometimes only skin deep.

THE PROBLEM OF PAPERWORK

Other forms of monitoring were more difficult to undermine or ignore. Bureaucratic requirements of the modern school and technological methods of monitoring teachers' work were more reliable than a human being and they weighed on teachers more heavily than even the intimidating supervisor. Teachers complained bitterly about the reams of paperwork assigned to them, including the regular recording of student attendance, health, and age statistics, truant officer reports, communication with parents, calculations of regular and final class averages and grade statistics, and annual documentation of teachers' professional and license accreditation. Clerks and secretaries were supposed to complete some of teachers' paperwork, but teachers complained that their schools had too few clerks. So severe was the problem that in 1922 the Teachers' Council recommended (in vain) that on the last four days of each term, students be sent home early so that teachers would have time to complete not only their grading but also the piles of end-of-term reports. New York teachers were not alone in their complaints: In 1926, the Department of Classroom Teachers of the National Education Association created a Committee on the Reduction of Clerical Work to address the problem that plagued the nation's teachers.[45]

Teachers disliked not only the amount of clerical work but also the disorder with which clerical tasks were assigned. They complained that demands for clerical work were brought into classrooms while they were teaching and that they were expected to be completed in unreasonably short periods of time and with a confusing amount of duplication. According to one teacher:

> In the last three weeks I have had at least six calls for records to be handed in within one, two, or three days after the notice, and sometimes requiring a considerable amount of research or writing—this just at the time of mid-term examinations and marks.[46]

Teachers were particularly resentful that much of the clerical work demanded of them was useless for the school and the students. Complaints about clerical work related directly to issues of teacher morale and undercut any image of professionalism among the teaching force. As one teacher complained:

> Why must everything, even the ordering of a needle, be done in duplicate and triplicate? Why should a high-priced teacher, supposedly an expert in her field, have to spend at least two-fifths of her time as a clerk?[47]

One English teacher at Wadleigh High School expressed her feelings about clerical work in a poem published in the Brooklyn Teachers Association Report of 1925. Dedicating her poem to the "Teachers of the World," the poet eased her frustration about clerical duties with humor. Notable also in the poem is the description of the teachers' clerical work as the kind of "toil" in the "mechanical grind" of the modern factory.

> All day long at the mechanical grind—
> Papers—Papers—Papers—
> I feel as if I could just lie down
> And die amid them all.
> Test papers to read,
> Time sheets to sign;
> Before I begin the day's toil,
> General notice No. 38 to read,
> A mimeographed blank to fill out,
> A package of yellow "exam" papers,
> A pile of sewing envelopes
> Two hundred weekly themes in lead pencil.
> No wonder the price of paper is high
> We use too much paper to live.
> Some day I know I'll die of it all.
> Then someone will write an obituary notice in a paper,
> And the school paper will print a full-length portrait of me
> Holding a paper in my hand.[48]

Another teacher dryly described New York City teachers as: "highly paid clerks who are capable of teaching when the reports and other things give us the requisite leisure." Although paperwork seemed endless to teachers, in the supervisory literature of the day paperwork was hardly mentioned as a problem with which teachers might need help or support. The intrusion of bureaucratic clerical tasks on teachers' workday seemed to be noticed only by teachers.[49]

result of the pressures of those broader working conditions. The effect of this working context shaped city teachers' ability to both open up and close off positive opportunities for student learning.

Historical studies of teaching have noted that no matter how many reformers propose pedagogical innovation, teachers' classroom work seems invulnerable to change. The classroom of the 1920s looked much like the classroom of earlier generations, with teachers dominating the room and delivering information to a passive student body. No matter how often reformers urged teachers to lead student-centered classrooms organized around student discussion, individual instruction, problem solving, and hands-on activities, teachers have overwhelmingly relied on teacher-centered practices of lecturing, textbook memorization, and standardized student performance. The reasons for teachers' stubborn resistance to change has been less clearly understood, in part because historians have observed the classroom in a vacuum, isolated from the context of teachers' other work. Furthermore, evidence of classroom activities of the past is fragmentary, consisting of only piecemeal snapshots of teachers' work. The historical "truth" of many teacher–student relations has been difficult to identify because the observer has often been a reminiscing student or teacher who told only one side of the story, or an investigator in search of evidence of "good" or "bad" teaching in a few observations. This narrow portrait of teachers' work has been reinforced by stereotypical images of teachers as either cruel taskmasters or paragons of child-centered creativity. The teacher is seen as a character who exists only at his or her desk at the front of the classroom and whose interactions with students occur with no relationship to the outside world.[2]

But teachers' work and their relationships with students are far more complex than the static image of classroom instruction, and their ability to teach is greatly affected by their working conditions. In the 1920s, the increased number of students and the diversity of those students, the expanded curricular expectations, and multiplied bureaucratic responsibilities left city teachers racing through the schoolday with little time to attend to students. Facing inconsistent guidelines for the classroom, many teachers created their own teaching methods, accommodating vague and contradictory regulations to their own needs in the classroom. Students played a central role in this creation of a patchwork of teaching methods, because students were both the subject of teachers' work and the tools for that work. Furthermore, although starkly separated by the power differential between them, teachers and students were strangely affiliated in their common experience of the school organization. Together in the classroom, hallways, and schoolyards, teachers and students wrestled with the broader demands of the school, and often with each other, negotiating the best way to complete their work.

SCHOOLS AND THE CHALLENGE OF YOUTH CULTURE

Children flooded the New York City public school system in the 1920s at an astounding rate. An average of 21,000 new students entered the school system every year during the decade. On the first day of school in 1922, the city's school enrollment peaked at 1 million, a total increase of more than 40,000 students over the previous year. Much of the enrollment increase was in the expanding outer boroughs: Manhattan's school population actually declined during the decade, while in the Bronx, Queens, and Brooklyn, the school registers increased by an average of 60,000 children in each borough. The main reasons for the increase were recent changes in child labor and compulsory education laws which extended the age of required school attendance to 18 and restricted the granting of work permits to children under that age. Most affected by these changes was the high school. The gradual tightening of child labor and compulsory education laws radically changed the role of the high school from an institution for a tiny elite to one servicing more than half of the adolescent population. At the same time, changes in the labor market in the 1920s made a high school diploma more valuable in the workplace. The expansion of white-collar work enticed more working-class families to keep their children in secondary school in order to earn the minimum requirements for work in the medical, clerical, and business fields. These variables drew into the schools an unprecedented array of students from working-class and ethnic backgrounds, changing the very character of the city high school. In the ninth-grade class at Erasmus Hall High School in Brooklyn in 1927, for example, more than half of the students were first-generation immigrants from homes where English and one other language were spoken.[3]

But schooling was still not a universal experience for all city children. In 1930 one-quarter of the New York City population aged 7 to 20 did not attend school. One reason for this was that city officials were clearly ambivalent about efforts to enforce compulsory education laws among the city's poorest residents. The board of education's attendance bureau was chronically underfunded and understaffed, and the number of factory inspectors in search of underage workers was equally tiny. Reformers were even less successful at regulating children who did piecework at home or other low-skilled work on the street. Nor did local schools help in reformers' efforts to require school attendance, since many principals and teachers discouraged working-class and immigrant students from attending school and local administrators certified illiterate, failing, or underage students simply to get them out of the system. Schools were already overcrowded, and many school officials were relieved to get rid of students who were themselves dragged unwillingly to school.[4]

Nor could revised laws convince all young people to voluntarily go to school when the city streets offered so many other exciting distractions. For middle- and working-class city children, immigrant and native-born alike, a New York City childhood was one spent twisting between traditional family expectations and modern urban youth culture. The vibrant culture of urban street life lured students into the modern marketplace of popular entertainment, including movie theaters, sidewalk stores, amusement parks, and dance halls. City streets were busy and sociable places, throbbing with traffic and trade, and rich with neighborhood culture. At lunchtime around city schools, children would take over the neighborhood, swarming around the hot dog vendors and lemonade, ice cream, and candy stands, racing around the sidewalks yelling at one another. Boys, in particular, joined gangs that asserted a tough street masculinity over the seemingly more feminine world of the school. One observer of the Jewish community of Brownsville remembered that even the "traditional Jewish passion" for education "fell apart under the violent impact of street life." A newly immigrated 10-year-old Italian boy was intimidated by the youth culture of his neighborhood in the Bronx, a place where, as he described it, "there were boys of all ages shooting dice on the streets and in the backyards, and small kids smoking cigarettes, playing cards for money out in the gutters, and worst of all, stealing." Other boys intimidated him, calling him a sissy because he kept off the street and wouldn't play craps. For young Harpo Marx, who left school after the second grade, the life of the street offered all the skills he needed, and, in comparison, "school was all wrong. . . . It didn't teach anybody how to exist from day to day, which was how the poor had to live."[5]

Social reformers observed these behaviors with increasing anxiety and proposed to integrate the school deeper into the community to counteract the social problems that they saw as so ingrained in the lives of modern city youth. The city slum was not merely "a grimy mass of brick and mortar," wrote one sociologist who studied New York City's bleakest neighborhoods in the 1920s and 1930s, it was also "a whole series of habits, attitudes, and sentiments, fixed within a mold of social organization and held together by the cement of economic adversity." The slum was "imprinted in the minds of those who occupy it, both adults and children." The school needed to take up the task of "conditioning and re-conditioning the child, directing his activities, and altering his behaviors." The instruction in habits, skills, common knowledge and values was the greatest task of the school in a chaotic city in uncertain social times.[6]

City schools of the 1920s were under orders to educate students in specific values and behaviors. Teachers were instructed to teach American values and citizenship, ignoring and often forcefully denying the foreign cultures of their students. The regular reading of the Pledge of Allegiance and the salute to the flag, the celebration of Christian holidays, and a curriculum of American history and civics created an environment that was foreign to most immigrant children or children from non-Christian faiths. The emphasis on silence, order, and cleanliness could instill fear and trembling in poor students who might be humiliated by their teachers for the most personal behaviors, such as not having a clean handkerchief, not wearing clean clothes, or being caught in morning inspection with a dirty neck or fingernails. New York City schools stressed oral exercises in pronunciation out of a concern that the quality of the English language was in decline due to the influx of immigrants, and teachers were expected to correct flawed accents, poor grammar, and slang in the attempt to achieve American cultural uniformity.[7]

Another way to socialize students was to divide them by behavior and ability into separate tracks, including ungraded classes for students who might be found "incorrigible," mentally deficient, "backward," or "laggards"; special open-air classrooms for physically impaired students with respiratory ailments; and high-level academic classes. Faith in tracking was undisputed in the board of education, which argued that grouping by ability allowed students to progress at their own speed and inspired slower students to push themselves into the more advanced group. Some of the justification for the tracking of students by ability was that it improved teachers' working conditions by making the classroom more homogeneous. In one of the few formal expressions of concerns for teachers' working conditions, New York City educators admitted that breaking the class into groups "lightens the teacher's labors," thereby allowing for better teaching. The Brooklyn Teachers' Association promoted the organization of disciplinary schools for pupils who were "depraved, vicious, or habitually lawless" specifically to ease teachers' disciplinary problems.[8]

The issue of controlling city students was addressed head-on in the promotion of classroom discipline. In the postwar years, strict discipline came back in vogue in New York City schools, reflecting a dissatisfaction with those progressive educators who had promoted an increased sympathy for children in child-centered classrooms and an emphasis on guidance over punishment. The extent to which such "child centeredness" had actually entered New York City public schools before World War I was minimal, but progressive ideas of laxity were a convenient source to blame for the chaos that was seen in city schools in the 1920s. The increase in school enrollments, and in the cultural diversity of those enrollments, furthered the image that schools were becoming increasingly undisciplined and in need of a return to rigorous authority. The message of school officials during the 1920s was of the necessity for closer supervision of students by teachers and of strict discipline in a particularly masculine and military manner. "You need

discipline in the teaching of students just as much as you do in the army,"
stated New York City Superintendent of Schools William O'Shea in 1926.
"They must be orderly and quiet before they can be taught." If the nation
really wanted "moral education," then people would soon "clamor for the
return of discipline to the schools," argued one writer. Disorder in schools
was thus identified as a result of relaxed teaching practices, not the increase
in school enrollments, class size, or the economic, linguistic, and ethnic diversity of students in New York City schools.[9]

The school of the 1920s, then, was intended to be an expansive social
service agency that controlled potentially delinquent urban youth; it was
also to be a civic educator intent on the Americanization of new immigrants,
a judge of character and native ability, and a cohesive and consistent disciplinarian of all students. The extent to which teachers were able to take on all
these objectives was another matter.

WHEN TEACHERS MET STUDENTS

City children brought their street behaviors, beliefs, and resistances to school
with them, and New York schools in the 1920s were rocked by incidences
of student riots, robberies, and murders. In the spring of 1922, students in
Brooklyn schools made glass bombs out of wartime military equipment and
exploded them in their classrooms. Teachers also met students in both elementary and secondary schools who were sexually promiscuous, chronic
liars, and troublemakers, as well as undernourished and poorly clothed
children exhausted from lives of poverty. Students appeared in class with
influenza, syphilis, tuberculosis, lice, the common cold, and other infectious
ailments. They dropped in and out of school, escaping the truant officer in
the city alleys, picking up odd jobs, joining gangs, and literally risking their
lives on the street, where an average of 42 New York City children a month
were accidentally killed by traffic.[10]

Teachers' responses to their students were influenced by a variety of different factors, including their own biography, the physical working conditions inside their schools, and the nature of their local administrative leadership. From the first day of school, the glaring differences between teachers
and their students could create a shaky foundation for future relations.
Many new teachers were clearly shocked by the diverse characteristics and
capabilities of the young people seated in their classrooms. Although most
New York City teachers had been born and educated in the city, and an
increasing number came from immigrant households, teachers were by and
large people who had achieved something akin to a middle-class status by

completing high school and teacher training school or college. Certainly teachers had spent a good many years learning how to be successful at formal schooling. Many were stunned to meet students who outrightly resisted school, whose academic backgrounds were meager, who might be poor, hungry, and unhealthy, and who were from ethnic, cultural, or religious backgrounds about which teachers had preconceived prejudices. A teacher's first encounter with such a student group might be especially disorienting in an overcrowded classroom of 40 students.

Furthermore, it was all but impossible for teachers to ignore students' social and personal problems when teaching, leaving some teachers to feel at a complete loss about how to approach their classroom work. A liberal arts graduate of Hunter College found herself totally unprepared for the academic limitations of her students at Harran High School, where working students attended school every other week and apprenticed at jobs in the alternating weeks. Early in her teaching, she was advised by her supervisor not to fail so many students.

> He said to me: "How do you react to failure?" Of course I hadn't had many failures: you didn't get to where I got by failing. So he said: "This is the first marking period and you've given this child a D and how do you think he is going to respond to this?" It was one piece of good advice I got. I had to realize that these people were not like me. These people didn't come equipped the way I came.[11]

Teachers found that teaching pronunciation was a daily task that interrupted other lessons. For teachers from immigrant backgrounds, this process was particularly poignant and emotionally draining. Anzia Yezierska described her own futile experiences trying to teach her students not to "murder the language as I did when I was a child of Hester Street."

> "Now, children, let's see how perfectly we can pronounce the words we went over yesterday."
> On the board I wrote, S-I-N-G.
> "Aby! Pronounce this word."
> "Sing-gha," said Aby.
> "Sing," I corrected.
> "Sing-gha," came from Aby again.
> "Rosy Stein! You can do better. Show [Aby] how to speak. Make a sentence with the word 'sing.'"
> "The boids sing-gha."
> "Rosy, say bird."
> "Boid," repeated small Rosy with great distinctness. "Boid."[12]

Teachers were encouraged to visit students' families in an attempt to understand students' background. But for many teachers, these visits only highlighted the gaping distance between their students' lives and their own. One teacher only learned the extent of her students' difficulties when she visited their homes and gained a sympathetic, if perhaps somewhat condescending, attitude.

> I never knew the true facts of life until I went to Harlem and saw how some of these children lived in these houses. You couldn't blame the children for not knowing what to do because their minds were full of all these awful things.[13]

Another teacher expressed doubts about visiting students' homes, sensing that teachers were stepping beyond their expertise into something they knew very little about, including the family's cultural background and intra-family relationships.[14]

> Very regularly I would go visit students at their homes. But I learned that this was not such a good thing to do because the picture got so big and you could only handle so much. After seeing the home, you could only see the child in the midst of his problems. Unless you are able to see the whole picture and treat it as the whole picture, then you can only take a little bit at a time.[15]

But some teachers from working-class or immigrant backgrounds could feel more affinity toward and understanding of students from similar backgrounds. Dorothy Meyer relied on her working-class immigrant background when she taught in a Harlem school.

> They began to show me that they were not there to learn. I discovered that the first morning. I said to them: Now I'm a new teacher and I'm not sure I know how to teach, but if any of you have a mother or father who is working and anybody tried to make them lose that job, what would you think of that person? . . . I'm like you, I told them: your parents need a job, and I need a job.[16]

The expectation that teachers socialize their students could give them free rein to express their own cultural biases. So unsupervised were teachers, and so undefined was the school system's understanding of different cultures, that teachers were essentially allowed to act out their prejudices in the classroom. One New York City teacher did just that when the Egyptian mother of her student spoke about how ugly America was in comparison to her native land. Realizing that the woman only knew New York's dreary Lower East Side, the teacher designed a year-long curriculum on "The Making of America" that examined the nation's European origins and American geography. Apparently, it did not occur to the teacher to take advantage of a native Egyptian's pride in her country. To this teacher, the object of American education was very simply to teach American culture, narrowly defined.[17]

Black students bore the most severe consequences of a hypocritical school system that promised equity but allowed bigotry. With the growth of the black population in Harlem, schools in the 1920s became increasingly segregated. Harlem schools were notoriously overcrowded, dilapidated, and poorly staffed. Because most black families were poor, many black students were forced to work after school and to take on housework and care of siblings. Limited local recreational facilities or parks, day nurseries, children's clubs, or settlement houses in Harlem also contributed to the poor academic performance of Harlem schoolchildren.[18]

Inside schools, black children faced additional problems. The predominance of black students in overcrowded and aging school buildings furthered the flight of white teachers from those schools and left those remaining teachers to deal with the most demanding working conditions. Nor was there a formal structure to prevent racist behavior in schools. For a number of years, the principal of the Manhattan Trade School for Girls was reported to have refused to admit qualified black students to the school, arguing that black girls had a "chip on their shoulder," were lazy, and made bad workers. Black parents organized to have a black guidance counselor, teacher Gertrude Ayer Johnson, appointed to the school, but she was not given a desk and was discouraged from meeting the school staff. Johnson reported what earlier investigators had found: While many white teachers encouraged their black students, they still held prejudicial views about black parents, whom they believed were too lazy to help their children. Some white teachers showed their misunderstanding of and disdain for black students more severely. At a predominantly black school in 1913, black parents accused teachers of inflicting excessive corporal punishment on students and of degrading students verbally. Teachers responded that students were uncontrollable without such strict punishment. In the eyes of many black students, such a school was hardly worth the effort. As one fictional black student was described in a novel by black teacher and poet Jessie Fauset: Peter "did not like school,—too many white people and consequently, as he saw it, too much chance for petty injustice." In a school system that barely trained teachers for their working conditions inside city schools and that avoided monitoring teachers' bigoted behavior, "petty injustice" to students was often the norm.[19]

TEACHERS AND THE PROBLEM OF CLASSROOM CONTROL

Teachers' most persistent problem in the classroom was discipline. Willard Waller, who observed schools in the late 1920s and early 1930s, identified teachers' urgent need for help with discipline matters when he described classrooms as veritable battlegrounds where teachers and students wrestled for control. He described the teacher–student relationship as a kind of "institutionalized dominance and subordination," with teachers' and students' interests in direct conflict. Because the conflict was never fully resolved, teachers' hold over their students was "constantly threatened by the students themselves." Waller suggested that the trauma of first losing control over a classroom radically transformed the new idealist teacher into an expert in social control. New teachers swiftly learned to take on the least humane characteristics of formal schooling. Empathy, flexibility, and creativity were in effect jolted out of teachers by the reality of the classroom. Regimentation, authoritarianism, and a fixation on behavior became the guiding precepts of the experienced classroom teacher. Randolph Bourne described a classroom teacher he observed in 1914 as a kind of neutralizer of student energy. In the monotonous daily classroom of recitations and lectures, students grasped wildly for any distraction to light up their frozen minds.[20]

> The most trivial incident assumed importance; the chiming of the town clock, the passing automobile, a slip of the tongue, a passing footstep in the hall, would polarize the wandering attention of the entire class like an electric shock. Indeed, a large part of the teacher's business seemed to be to demagnetize, by some little ingenious touch, his little flock into their originally inert and static elements.[21]

So much did teachers dread the loss of classroom control that they responded to students' active disturbances in the classroom more than to passive students. A study of teachers in Cleveland and Minneapolis in the 1920s found that students' overt types of behavior, assaults on teachers' authority, and annoying and disturbing actions could lead teachers to a kind of counterattack as they wrestled for dominance in the classroom. Teachers' responses could take a variety of forms, the most notorious of which was the sheer wielding of authority by intimidation and punishment. Many New York City teachers were known to lead strict classrooms where talking was prohibited, only assigned reading was allowed, and students were punished in front of their classmates for incorrect answers. Teachers' use of physical force, intimidation, and humiliation was remembered grimly by students as the worst and most memorable part of their education.[22] Recalled one former student:

My first-grade teacher, she was part of the old school; she was the kind of teacher who walked up and down the aisle. She looked like a witch, and she would walk around with a ruler in her hand. We were supposed to be looking at our book and I had another book besides that book and she came behind me, I didn't see her, and she hit me in the hand, actually cut my hand with the ruler, my hand was bleeding.[23]

New teachers were particularly aware of their fragile hold over their classrooms. One teacher who began teaching elementary school in Queens in the late 1920s remembered:

When I was a new teacher I used to stand up in front of the class and think: if only those kids knew what they could do to me. What if I told them to put away their books and they didn't? What would I do?[24]

For new high school teachers, classroom control was especially difficult since the students might be only a few years younger than the teachers themselves. When a young woman teacher faced a class of teenage boys, there was a particular need for fast and creative thinking. Margaret Jamer began teaching biology to a group of 18-year-old students who plagued her with spit balls.

As I was writing on the blackboard I could feel the spit balls going zip zip zip. I knew who had done it so I turned around very quickly and said: "Al, tomorrow I'm going to challenge you to a fight and we'll see who controls this class." I came home and my younger brother taught me to shoot spit balls. We stayed up all night. The next day I put a big target up on the blackboard and I hit the center every time.[25]

Just as the contest was ending, Jamer's principal entered the classroom and called her into his office to account for her behavior. Fortunately for Jamer, the principal understood the reasoning behind her method and allowed Jamer to continue with the class, which, after that day, was far more respectful of their teacher. She had won their respect.

Teachers developed other strategies for negotiating peace with students. One teacher literally bought off her most disruptive student in a class of surly and inattentive boys who were attending school only in hopes of earning their working papers as soon as possible.

I come into the class and it's a class full of boys, some of them bigger than I am. . . . They began to show me that they were not there to learn.

I discovered that the first morning. . . . One was very tough and he was much bigger than I: he wanted to be noticed, he wanted the attention and not the teacher. I offered him a job as my secretary. I told him: For every day that the class accepts me, I will give you a nickel. To anybody that was out of order he would walk up in that lumbering kind of way and crack his knuckles.[26]

For another teacher who was forced to bribe a student leader, the experience was demeaning because it implied that she did not have enough authority on her own. She remembered: "I had to take that kind of menial position. They were afraid of him and he kept [them] quiet in the classroom."[27]

For all the official emphasis on a "return to discipline," teachers received minimal advice about how to actually address discipline problems in the classroom. Teachers recorded rare visits from supervising administrators who were themselves overburdened by the enormity of their jobs and were often able to spend no more than a few minutes a year supervising each teacher. Nor had teacher education presented many useful guides to the realities of the classroom. New fields of study in educational psychology, child development, and mental hygiene placed a new emphasis on student learning styles and a decreased emphasis on the context of the classroom. Educational researchers and psychologists urged teachers to concentrate on developing long-term educational skills, and they critiqued teachers' apparently simple-minded obsession with immediate classroom problems such as discipline. Thus, at the same time that classroom discipline was emphasized by public officials, teacher educators urged teachers to focus on nurturing individual students' learning. The emphasis was on individual teachers' acts to elicit the proper student response, not on the context of the classroom. In the end, teachers were still evaluated on their control of the classroom, however, not just on learning outcomes.

The issue of corporal punishment cut to the heart of organizational problems in schools where individual teachers were held accountable for the failures of the school system. Corporal punishment was technically illegal, but under the by-laws of the board of education, teachers and principals were allowed to use force if administered with "reasonableness," *in loco parentis*. The identification, charging, and punishment of a New York City teacher for inflicting corporal punishment was unusual; once or twice a year during the 1920s a principal or teacher would be fined or suspended for regularly "boxing" or "attacking" a student, or for excessively mistreating students by leaving them outside in the playground in the rain. Of the 24 teachers fired from New York City schools between 1921 and 1926, only one was accused of inflicting corporal punishment. More teachers were reprimanded for *not* maintaining effective discipline than for inflicting corporal punishment, and teachers' inability to maintain discipline was also cause for dismissal or punishment. Teachers thus stood in the middle of a poorly defined and highly emotional issue. Society's ambivalence about corporal punishment was exemplified by the fact that in the 20 years before the 1920s, social reformers and child welfare advocates had made corporal punishment a primary public issue of the day. In the postwar period, however, the public outcry against child abuse and corporal punishment had diminished, in part due to the increased emphasis on traditional discipline. Indicative of public priorities was the fact that during the 1920s, laws were enacted to protect students from teachers' political views but not from their physical actions.[28]

Where incidences of corporal punishment were identified, it was explained by public commentators as the problem of a deviant individual, the extreme response of an inadequate teacher who had failed in both methods and morals. In a 1929 symposium on corporal punishment in a national education journal, one contributor argued that "when teachers revert back to cave man tactics they declare their own weakness." According to a second commentator, the use of corporal punishment was a clear sign of an inadequate teacher, "an index of poor methods and techniques and of lack of originality and resourcefulness." The teacher who resorted to such actions was admitting to laziness, indifference, and sheer disrespect for the child. Such a teacher admitted by his or her actions that: "I can not take this child with me in my efforts on his behalf. I have not been able to meet him on his own level and build up his experiences. I have not exerted myself to know why he reacts as he does and have neither the time nor the inclination to study this child sufficiently to familiarize myself with his characteristics."[29]

Discussions about the sin of resorting to harsh discipline were directed primarily at women, not only because of the predominance of women in the occupation but also because of a perceived weakness on the part of women in handling discipline problems. Ironically, the very feminine qualities that were expected to create nurturing environments were criticized as the source of poor discipline. The instruction and management of children was "nervous work," and according to popular ideology about women's capabilities, women were nervous creatures. The overworked woman teacher was seen as a threat to classroom order, drained as she was by home responsibilities, feminine health, emotional sensitivity, and the inevitable strain of the working world. "Teaching wears on women more than upon men," argued one educator, because in times of classroom stress a woman teacher "is apt to fall back on her nerve force, of which she has generally little to spare."[30]

Discipline problems were thus identified as the fault of the individual woman teacher's feminine physiology, and the solution was also up to the individual teacher, who was advised to concentrate on improving her own personal life, health, and humor to avoid "frayed out nerves," to stay healthy and relaxed, to develop a positive and cheerful attitude about life, and to take up interests outside the classroom. Discipline was apparently never a problem for the teacher who was herself "a vivacious, interesting human," asserted a midwestern teacher to her colleagues, and at any hint of a discipline problem, the teacher was advised to "take the blame yourself, for there it can rightly be placed." Classroom management was thus presented as an individual responsibility that reflected immediately on a woman's gendered identity. Women teachers were taught that the struggle to keep classroom order was mirrored by their own attempts to maintain their own personal moral order and to retain their own identity as self-restrained, rational, but still caring women.[31]

The heavily moralized pressure against corporal punishment did not mean that teachers stopped relying on this ultimate method of discipline. Rather, as teachers in New York City schools observed, corporal punishment existed regularly in schools, but on subterranean levels. The vague regulation and definition of corporal punishment furthered this complicated situation, as many teachers who themselves disapproved of corporal punishment were able to convince themselves that they were not in fact inflicting it. Teachers looked to one another for strategies to sidestep official and pro forma regulations about corporal punishment as they tried to mediate between official proscriptions of their job, the stressful realities of controlling a class of 40 children, and their own conscience about good teaching. By drawing their own line of what was acceptable discipline, teachers calculated that they were free from a legal charge of inflicting corporal punishment, and they eased their own personal anxiety about their fall from the role of the nurturing teacher.

Some teachers relied on the threatening image of the cruel teacher as a substitute for actual physical punishment. One teacher developed a theory that "teaching is seventy percent discipline and thirty percent education. . . . If you don't have enough iron, you can't manage. The kids have to suspect something; nobody will hit you, but the idea is that something is hanging over you so you have got to behave yourself. If you can get that across, then you can teach something." Another retired teacher remembered a colleague who used to say to her students: "'If you don't behave, I'll put you in the dictionary!' And they didn't know what a dictionary was, so they'd be terrified."[32] Teachers also received tips from their principals about how to maintain discipline through threats. One teacher remembered:

> I had one really difficult girl and [my principal] said to me: "There's only one thing to do: at three o'clock take her into another room with a ruler in your hand. And if she tells her parents, you can tell them that you don't teach in that room." . . . So I took this little girl into a room on the

fifth floor and I said: "See this ruler? If you annoy me, you'll get a lot of black and blue marks." It scared the daylights out of the girl going all the way up to that room and she didn't cause any more trouble.[33]

For the occasional student who got on a teacher's nerves one time too many, the threat of corporal punishment might ease the teacher's strain. One teacher remembered that with such a student, "I'd give him a little push on the behind and say: Want to take a walk with me after three o'clock?" Some teachers found backhanded ways to inflict punishment, and they learned to delineate force from actual "hitting," which they considered to be crossing the line into corporal punishment. Teachers were known to step on their students' toes "by accident," hit students with a pointer or ruler, shake students, or slap those who walked in the back of a line or in the chaos of a fire drill. The difference between "shaking" and "hitting" a student seemed significant to one teacher, who recalled: "Once I did take a child and shake him so his head hit the blackboard, and I was so terrified I couldn't sleep all night. But I refused to hit them."[34]

Cultural differences between parents and teachers were often illustrated in different attitudes toward corporal punishment. Teachers realized the irony of disciplining students without hitting them when some students were accustomed to their parents' use of physical force to maintain discipline at home. Teachers tried to negotiate this seeming contradiction by separating home behavior from school behavior. One teacher remembered a student's father who came to school carrying a switch. "He wanted me to hit the kid. I said: I'm not paid to hit him. If you want to hit him, *you* hit him."[35] In such instances, teachers recognized the tenuous hold they had over their students' lives and the extent to which they had to protect themselves from becoming too involved, even with students for whom they felt affection and responsibility. Such feelings of helplessness and lack of control showed teachers all too clearly how the realities of the urban school punctured the image of the school as a rational place with humane intentions.

Teachers also understood that the best source of discipline was an administration that backed up the teacher.

> On the whole the kids were good. One of the reasons they were good was that . . . we had a very strong Assistant Principal and she would back the teachers completely as long as they were within the law. The children knew that if they did not behave their parents would be called for. I never had as good an Assistant Principal. . . . I knew that any child that I sent outside my classroom door wouldn't leave.[36]

But such support was unusual, and most teachers were forced to respond to their work in an independent manner, often blaming themselves for their failures with classroom management. "Everything that went wrong was simply because I lacked experience," remembered one teacher about her own education in learning to discipline students. Having been taught that such a problem was her *own* problem, this teacher learned to rely on her own wits and to draw on her own personal resources. Learning how to be a teacher meant learning how to maintain one's own independent response to the classroom. As one teacher remembered: "I became a pretty good disciplinarian but nobody helped me; I looked around and I saw what was going on and I took the best that I saw."[37]

Because teachers were forced to rely on surreptitious practices, self-denial, and personal justifications as they struggled with student discipline, the problem of classroom management was drawn out of the purview of the formal school organization. School management was relieved of the burden of what happened in the classroom and free to concentrate on the less emotionally murky issues of curriculum, financing, and public sector politics. If classroom discipline was not seen as a problem caused, in part, by oversized classes, inadequate working conditions, and insufficient support and guidance for teachers, then classroom discipline must be the responsibility of the teacher alone. For teachers, the paramount and basic question of how to maintain classroom control was an emotionally laden, terribly lonely, and contradictory issue. Classroom discipline problems were forever only teachers' problems.

THE CLIMATE OF THE CLASSROOM

For many teachers and students, school was simply not a pleasant place to spend one's days. Randolph Bourne's 1914 painful description of his return to his old high school reminds us of the predominant experience of most students in American schools in any generation. As he sat down in his old seat, Bourne felt "that queer sense of depression, still familiar after ten years, that sensation, in coming into the schoolroom, of suddenly passing into a helpless, impersonal world, where expression could be achieved and curiosity asserted only in the most formal and difficult way." The boredom was endemic, leading some students to disrupt the "peacefully dragging recitation" and another to distract himself for an hour sharpening his pencil. Here, in the "artificial atmosphere" of the classroom, these actions took on a kind of symbolic quality, an "assertion against stupid authority, a sort of blind resistance against the attempt of the schoolroom to impersonalize him."[38]

Agnes De Lima's observation of a fourth-grade class in New York City in 1924 paints a similarly depressing portrait of the most confining and spiritless education. By fourth grade, these students were already apparently numbed to their situation.

> They sat there, this spring morning, sunk in apathy, not one of them by even so much as a shuffle venturing to rebel openly against the accustomed regime. One boy, to be sure, instead of working his sums was, under cover of his hand, scribbling a series of ciphers across his paper, and another was stealthily watching the meaningless performance in awed fascination.

The students droned their recitations in "utter indifference." They moved blankly through their physical exercises like "wooden dolls moved by a master hand." Indeed, as lunchtime neared, the class "seemed past any possibility of life." But when the noon bell rang, "a shiver of expectancy went over the room." The teacher methodically directed the students to rise to get their coats in order, torturing the children with suspense until every boy stood perfectly still in line. Finally, she let the boys go into the hall, in properly formed lines, met by other lines presided over by similarly "glaring guardians." Only at the downstairs door, as the children entered the street, was vigilance relaxed and "the children burst out into the free air of the streets like so many exploding shells." Or as Randolph Bourne observed of the end of the school day, "Everything suddenly became human again. The brakes were off, and life, with all its fascinations of intrigue and amusement, was flowing once more."[39]

Yet for all the inherent conflict, teachers and students maintained a strange symbiotic relationship in schools. Both groups were stuck in the same classroom, and the same building, and under many of the same structures and rules for days on end throughout the year. And in spite of the tensions and strains of the city classroom, some teachers described their relationships with students as one of the primary benefits of their work. Through the muddle of school regulations, the problems that urban children brought to school, and the stresses inherent in the teacher–student relationship, teachers found that the excitement of teaching could still thrive. While many teachers were overwhelmed by the task before them and simply did the minimum by maintaining classroom control, other teachers negotiated their ambivalent position as disciplinarian, social worker, and academic instructor and devised ways of engaging their students.

For many city students, the classroom could be a refuge from a demanding and dangerous outside world or the source of the intellectual and emotional stimulation that was absent at home. One former New York City student from a working-class household remembered that "school was a place I wanted to go to. . . . It was a symbol of order, it was a symbol of structure and it was a symbol of important things to learn." Some children found pleasure in the school precisely because it offered them relief from either the peer pressure of the street of the restrictive traditionalism of family. If they were lucky, such students would come to a school where teachers were able to respond to them just as eagerly.[40]

For those teachers who had the self-confidence, skills, and amenable working conditions, the experience of teaching students compensated for the confusion outside the classroom door. For many teachers, the students were the most rewarding part of their job and it was in their interest to engage their students and make the schoolday pleasant and productive. As a midwestern English teacher wrote to *The English Journal* in 1928, teaching was often dry and dreary work that sapped the imagination of thoughtful people until the unexpected student made it all worthwhile.

> Rebelliously, I glare about at themes,
> And contract papers, quizzes and reports
> That dull my mind, and wreak me out of sorts . . .
> This, teaching? Is there nothing that redeems?
>
> My class pours in. A sonnet I've been reading
> Lies there before me. Would they understand?
> Majestic, brave, the lines roll on—and cease.
> A quick response in young hearts oft unheeding
> Brings murmurs of "I love that!" There's been fanned
> A flame. From teaching who would wish release?[41]

Teachers also empathized with students about long and dreary study periods and doubted their own role as monitor. Remembering their own days as students, teachers felt the restlessness of the endless schoolday, the more grueling periods of testing, or the torture of being locked inside the classroom on a warm spring afternoon. One teacher from New Jersey described her students during a test, and the

> Shuffle of papers, bowed heads, and driving pens;
> Silence, then rattle of papers again, and a boy's restless feet on the floor . . .
> Jane's pencil is running before her, over her practice paper.
> "I'm glad I studied that"; I can almost hear her say it . . .

As the teacher watched, she shared her students' concern about passing and failing. Remembering her own days as a student, the teacher wondered if she had properly prepared her class for the test.[42]

Another teacher from Philadelphia saw her own girlhood self in her students and remembered the free and active life of her rural childhood. Regretfully, she now watched her students as they sat "primly" in rows, their "docile pens record the stupid words my dull lips say." Still another teacher recorded her ambivalent impressions of a Friday afternoon class in the spring as that of a "monotone" waiting for a reprieve.[43]

A New York City teacher expressed the ambivalence of the upcoming summer vacation when, after months of "cultivating strangers" like a gardener trimming plants, painfully applying twine, knives, and clippers, she could now only hope to prepare them for their future, "only try to fertilize them well, and pray for rain." One teacher privately responded to friends' concerns and "jeers" that she was sacrificing all adventure in her life by sitting with "those dumb kids." Little do they know, she wrote, of the excitement and rewards of teaching young children.[44] As an urban teacher wrote of her students:

> Oh little, grumbling clowns, you will
> Never guess, from day to day,
> The secret, chuckling dancing thrill
> That comes, when thus I draw my pay![45]

The classroom could take on a life of its own with its own social dynamics, a steady anchor of daily rhythms, requirements, expectations, and personal interactions. Elementary school teachers, in particular, spent the bulk of their working days in one room with their students, and if only for this reason, many teachers maintained distinctly personal and intense relationships with their students. Teachers were often personally affected by students' accomplishments. More than 60 years after it happened, Alice Marsh remembered one of her most exciting experiences as a teacher when a boy realized that he could read after six weeks of not understanding a thing.

> He would sing along but he didn't know what that said up there. He never understood what was going on, apparently. . . . In the afternoon we read the primer, . . . the kids used to get up and read. So that if Johnny followed the page and he heard Jimmy reading it, he was doing something. This little Peter sat there and somebody was reading and he said: "I can read!" Just like that, he blurted right out. So the other kid stopped, of course, all the kids stopped—who ever yelled out like that in class? So I said: Well, that's fine Peter, let's see you do it. And the other kid sat down and Peter stood up and sure enough, he read. And I said to him: How about the next page, you think you can read the next page? And he turned the page and said: "Yes! Yes I can!" Well, that was such a shock to me and to all the other kids, because here's this kid sitting here for six weeks not saying a word, but somehow it was like a jigsaw

puzzle and he made the connection and the whole thing burst. It was really a very exciting moment and I remember it all these years with such joy.[46]

Some teachers admitted that in their first year of teaching they learned how to teach from their students. Facing a classroom of strangers, many new teachers were especially relieved to find students with whom they could identify and make friends. When Sarah Cousins first began teaching high school theater and English, she found the older faculty and the working-class student body at Eastern District very different from her own upbringing. She became friends with one student and his family.

I was sometimes invited for Friday night dinners [with the family]. They were very bright people who were connected with the arts. It was a privilege to learn how to be a teacher from them.[47]

Teachers sometimes bonded with students in opposition to administrators. At Curtis High School in Staten Island, teachers came to students' defense when a student was reprimanded by the principal for throwing a snowball and when students tried to form a riding club over the objections of the principal. In both cases, teachers took a position between the formal authority of the principal and students' powerless position. Taking the position of informal advocate or club advisor, teachers were able to temporarily abandon their more formal role of school employee.[48]

Some teachers seem to have welcomed the maternal warmth and affection that could arise from working with small children. Some women elementary teachers hugged their students, praising them warmly and visiting their family's household. In both elementary and secondary schools, teachers befriended students, offering advice and encouragement in their studies and inviting them to after-school events. By encouraging good scholarship and interest in school work, teachers were indirectly improving their own jobs and adding an important personal element to their teaching. Those who gave their favorite students gifts of notebooks or who allowed good students to clean the blackboard were in a sense wooing their students to support them by encouraging good behavior. Teachers may also have appreciated the attention and admiration of fawning students. At times, the boundaries between favorite student and unpaid teacher's aide became thin as teachers appointed "proctors" to monitor classes while they stepped out, asked students to keep track of their clerical work, or lobbied students to participate in their planned activities.[49]

Teachers' emotional connections with students were furthered by the sense that the two groups were bonded together in the class. Both were subject to school rules, to examinations and evaluations, and to the criticisms of parents, administrators, and the community. Teachers, however, had to maintain authority in the classroom in order to get their job done; thus teachers had to walk a line between maintaining control over students and retaining the student loyalty and support that made the teaching day worthwhile. Dealing with individual students in individual classrooms, teachers learned that generalized rules and standard teaching methods were not always successful and that teachers had to contribute their own personal ingenuity to difficult classroom situations.

CONCLUSION

"Today, everybody is going to school," wrote Superintendent of Schools William O'Shea in his annual report of 1924–25. Furthermore, he added, everybody looked to the public school to resolve society's social and moral problems, as well as its educational deficiencies. In New York City in the 1920s, the great expectations of the public schools were strained by the sheer enormity of the school population and the diversity of abilities and needs of modern city students. Because "everybody" was in school, the school had to deal with "everybody's" problems.[50]

Schools were filled with students from a wide variety of ethnic and class backgrounds who brought to school all the problems of modern urban youth. The mission of New York City schools in the 1920s was to address all these problems while teaching a broad academic curriculum. Social reformers agreed that it was up to the classroom teacher to successfully engage all urban students so that they would willingly chose to follow one civic and moral standard, to learn about healthy and responsible living, to prepare for an adult life of productivity, and still to do their homework. These gargantuan goals were entangled in a large city school bureaucracy that haphazardly supervised more than 600 different city schools. Given the challenges presented by city students in the postwar era and the problems of the school bureaucracy, some teachers did accomplish all that was asked of them, but many others did not. Some observers of New York City schools told stories of the exceptional teacher who single-handedly inspired a failing student, but others described cold, unfeeling teachers who terrorized students with harsh punishments and mechanical lessons. Both existed in the huge city school system designed to address the multiple needs of more than 1 million students and the multiple demands of school and social reformers.

The persistent emphasis on the individual teacher's personal responsibility intensified a situation that promised standardized order but delivered chaos. The school system was allowed to pass the blame on to the teacher, ignoring its own responsibility to provide safe and sensible working conditions and supports for students and teachers. A teacher was supposed to be a "naturally" caring advisor and role model for students, and any deviation from that image was described as an individual phenomenon and a pathology, a solitary aberration, the result of a weak, poorly trained, or inadequate teacher. Teachers' experiences of discipline problems, and the conditions that furthered those problems, were thus effectively privatized and silenced behind classroom doors and within individual teachers' consciences.[51]

In a celebrated case that ran in the New York City press in the mid–1920s, a woman teacher was suspended from the public school system and committed to an insane asylum for appearing in a "bathrobe" in front of her class and for, on one occasion, saying to her classroom of students: "This is a hell of a class." (The teacher successfully sued the state for the commitment to the asylum and was reinstated.) The message was clear: Any teacher who broke down under the pressure of teaching was not a victim of difficult working conditions but was, simply, insane.[52] Teachers were expected to remain self-controlled and self-contained in their own classrooms, designing individual methods of getting through the schoolday, whether or not those methods benefited students.

Epilogue:
The Legacy of Teachers' Experience

As I WAS FINISHING this manuscript, I reread a classic novel about New York City schools. Bel Kaufman's *Up the Down Staircase*, first published in 1964, is the story of a young, inexperienced teacher working in "the maelstrom of an average city high school, where, inundated with trivia in triplicate, she had to cope with all that is frustrating and demeaning in the school system while dealing with larger human issues." Kaufman's goal for her book, which she drew from her own experiences as a New York City teacher, was to "show the lack of communication all the way down the line," including nonsensical administrative orders and irritating bureaucratic requirements. Emerging from the chaos of urban school administration was the persistent struggle of teachers to make sense out of their day. The style of this remarkable book showed just that: The text is composed entirely of official school memos, student papers, scribbles, doodles, and the notes that the teacher sends and receives from her colleagues in the same building, pleading for advice, offering support, crying frustration, and sharing the gallows humor of an absurd working situation.[1]

The fact that Kaufman's book was reprinted in 1991 indicates, much as this book about the 1920s does, that city teachers' experiences at work have changed little over the decades. Since I left New York City five years ago, my parents have sent me weekly clippings from the *New York Times* about overcrowded and dilapidated school facilities, confusing curricula, and desperate student problems. The recurrence of these problems should lead us to do more than shake our heads in amazement at the constancy of the ages. Teachers have been talking about why schools don't work for generations. Our obligation is to listen to what they say.

What kinds of questions can we ask teachers today that could offer the kind of insights that this book presents from teachers of the past? What could today's teachers tell us about what they experience, need, and hope for their workplace, and how might we design school reform initiatives to accommodate those experiences so that we can support, rather than restrict, teachers' work?

Few contemporary school reforms *do* address the needs or experiences of teachers. Business-supported reforms that propose national performance goals, technological innovations, and the production of skilled and trained future workers barely take into account teachers' ability to accomplish these tasks given their working conditions. Reform policies that restructure the school organization to incorporate teachers, parents, and the community are more promising, but only if, in fact, teachers are given authority.[2] Whatever their objectives, few of these reforms are initially generated in the school building by teachers or followed through by working teachers.

Nor have teacher-run organizations been able to adequately address the needs of their membership, primarily because teacher unions have been restricted by legal doctrine to address only certain issues in the school. Collective bargaining agreements are designed to primarily address wages and hours, thus excluding teacher unions from contributing to those areas that directly shape teachers' working conditions, such as class size, selection of materials, and methods of evaluation. Recent union contracts that encourage more union contributions to school policy run the risk of compromising union authority on those basic bread-and-butter issues, such as salary, that collective bargaining has assured teachers. Whatever their platform and leverage, teacher unions are rarely allowed to organize the appropriate solution to the complex problems that teachers face in their daily work.[3]

Teachers' own proposals for change have been difficult to read and are often widely divergent. For example, New York City teachers in the 1920s criticized the way in which the centralized school bureaucratic structure restricted their classroom teaching, yet at the same time they relied on that structure for their job rights and privileges. They also advocated small, locally controlled schools, while expressing frustration with the provinciality of local school management. They criticized the absence of supervisory support at the same time that they denounced what they believed to be too much supervision. Teachers' underground networks of teaching tips, which provided a cooperative source of survival mechanisms, could be very uncooperative and exclusive, since locally based teacher networks could effectively alienate teachers from different backgrounds or with opposing views, and could counteract the most progressive of school reforms.

That teachers' accounts of their work are complex and contradictory should not surprise us, given the nature of their work. According to teachers, their working conditions extend far beyond the classroom and include far more than curriculum, facilities, and educational goals and objectives. The most trivial classroom events make up the fabric of teachers' daily work. The distractions of a warm spring day, the excitement of a passing fire engine, the problems raised by a sick child, a spitball, or a special assembly, and the regularly rambunctious behavior of children require teachers to work on a moment-to-moment basis, ready to adapt, accommodate, and improvise at the drop of a hat. City teachers' work is traditionally high-pitched and frenetic as they address the planned needs and unplanned demands of the children in front of them and the school administration behind them. The immediacy of teachers' work, the need for on-the-spot problem solving, and the high intensity of the classroom means that, at the very minimum, teachers need strong but flexible support in their workplace.

Good school leadership consists of making the immediate issues of the schoolhouse central and then incorporating them into the goals of the workday, as well as providing adequate supplies, safe and clean facilities, consistent curriculum goals, and auxiliary support staff. Effective school leaders need to take into account the great variety of factors that affect teachers' work and to guide or mediate those factors for the sole purpose of improving teachers' ability to get their job done. School reform needs to be addressed *to* teachers' needs, respecting the legacy of their experiences at work.

Notes

INTRODUCTION

1. My understanding of work culture draws on the following: Kanpol, 1988; Montgomery, 1979; Benson, 1988; Melosh, 1982; di Leonardo, 1985. For discussions of work culture in other feminized occupations, such as clerical and restaurant work see Creighton, 1982; Barker & Downing, 1980; Kanter, 1977.

2. Waller, 1932, p. 375.

3. Teaching was always the most professional of all the jobs employing women until 1940, when secretarial work became the job employing the second-highest number of women. Between 1870 and 1930, the main occupations employing women were, in order, domestic work, agriculture, seamstresses, and laundresses (Hooks, 1947). Discussions on feminist perspectives on the history of teachers include Clifford, 1989; Weiler, 1989; Prentice & Theobald, 1991.

4. Finkelstein, 1989; Cuban, 1993; Silberman, 1993. For a recent analysis of reformers' seemingly endless attempts to reinvent teaching, see Tyack & Cuban, 1995.

5. Callahan, 1970; Tyack, 1974; Apple, 1989. For a recent commentary on the problem of business's misplaced reforms on schools, see Taggart, 1995.

6. Major works on the history of American teacher unions are Urban, 1982; Murphy, 1990. See also Quantz, 1985, for an analysis of why one group of teachers did not organize in the 1930s.

7. Goodlad, 1984, p. 28.

8. My approach to oral history was guided by some of the following: Spradley, 1979; Quantz, 1992; Rinehart, 1983. See also Ben-Peretz, 1995.

9. Quoted in "Lays Mania for Facts as Bane of Education," 1928.

10. Quoted in McManis, 1916, pp. 210–211.

CHAPTER 1

1. Freeman et al., 1992, pp. 219–267.

2. Kaestle, 1973; Ravitch, 1988.

3. Tyack, 1974.

4. Rice, 1969, pp. 29–54.

5. Mirel, 1993; Hammack, 1973, p. 328; Rice, 1969, p. 48.

6. School Survey Committee, 1924, p. 1161.

7. Quoted in Ravitch, 1988, p. 156.

8. Hammack, 1973; Urban, 1982, pp. 25–43.

9. Gruenberg, 1912, p. 90; Memorandum submitted by Various Teachers Associations, 1915; "The Case Against Efficiency," 1916.

10. Cremin, 1964, pp. 153–160; R. Cohen & Mohl, 1979; Ravitch, 1988, pp. 219–230.

11. Mayman, 1917, p. 84; Tyack, 1974, p. 250; Callahan, 1970.

12. Fraser, 1989; Urban, 1982.

13. Haley, 1904, p. 148.

14. P. Carter, 1992; Doherty, 1979.

15. Alexander, 1910, pp. 5–27; Wattenberg, 1936, pp. 41–66; High School Teachers' Association, 1921, pp. 21, 86.

16. Schlocklow, 1914–15; Locke, 1914–15, p. 23.

17. P. Carter, 1992, pp. 47–48.

18. Urban, 1982, pp. 90–91, 104–108; Muraskin, 1981.

19. Fahey, 1919; Tildsley, 1920.

20. Quoted in Buchholz, 1931, pp. 147–148.

21. Beale, 1936; Pierce, 1926, pp. 301–305.

22. *Brooklyn Teachers' Association Forty-Sixth Annual Report* (1919–20), p. 6.

23. Urban, 1982.

24. Rodgers, 1978, p. 47.

25. Edwards, 1979, pp. 91–98; Derber, 1966; Montgomery, 1987, pp. 4–24.

26. Ettinger, 1919, p. 6 ; Russell, 1920; Updegraff, 1922, p. 787; "Unionizing Teachers," 1919.

27. Bogan, 1919; Churchill, 1916, p. 14; Palmer, 1919.

28. Ortman, 1923, pp. 22, 78–79; quoted in Beale, 1936, p. 366.

29. McAuliffe, 1920; Gross, 1917.

30. E. F. Young, 1901; Bashaw, 1986, p. 366; Weiner, 1992.

31. Linville, 1924.

32. Lefkowitz, 1924; Teachers' League of New York City, 1914.

33. Teachers' Council, 1928, pp. 6–7.

CHAPTER 2

1. Waller, 1932, p. v.

2. Patri, 1925.

3. Desmond, 1919, p. 7; Still, 1956, p. 297. The 1920s are one of the most written about and analyzed decades because, as Lynn Dumenil (1995) notes, they marked the cultural emergence of the "modern era." See Frederick Allen's (1931) classic reflections, *Only Yesterday: An Informal History of the 1920s.* Ann Douglas's (1995) monumental study, *Terrible Honesty: Mongrel Manhattan in*

the 1920s, focuses on the cultural heart and rhythms of New York City in this period.

4. Maller, 1938, p. 166; Horowitz & Kaplan, 1959, p. 15; Graves, 1934, p. 32.

5. Osofsky, 1966; J. W. Johnson, 1940, pp. 3–4.

6. May, 1980, p. 164; Still, 1956, p. 264.

7. Maller, 1938, pp. 135–138; Board of Education of the City of New York, 1948, pp. 67–69, 86–87.

8. Board of Education of the City of New York, 1948, pp. 86–87; "Former Teachers as Government Employees," 1921; Fahey, 1919; "The Crisis in Education," 1920; "Report of Resignations of Teachers During Calendar Year 1919," 1920.

9. Coxe, 1931, pp. 8–9; Tildsley, 1932, p. 15; Citizen's Committee on Teachers' Salaries, 1927; Board of Education of the City of New York, 1948, pp. 110–111; Dumenil, 1995, pp. 56–97. For a larger survey of teachers' salaries and benefits in the United States through the twentieth century, see S. B. Carter & Savoca, 1992, and Sedlak & Schlossman, 1987.

10. Nifenecker, 1936, p. 197; Olneck & Lazerson, 1974; Counts, 1922.

11. D. M. Brown, 1987, p. 81; Berrol, 1976; Rury, 1991.

12. Markowitz, 1993, pp. 22–24; Murphy, 1990, pp. 23–45.

13. Rury, 1989; Sedlak & Schlossman, 1987.

14. Salaries in City School Systems, 1926–7, 1927; S. B. Carter, 1989; S. B. Carter & Prus, 1982; Breckinridge, 1972, pp. 167–214; Reverby, 1987, p. 98; Cott, 1987, pp. 132–134.

15. Joseph, 1994; Simmons, 1920.

16. "Spring Vacation," 1925.

17. Coffman, 1911; Hollis, 1929, pp. 205–206; McGuffey, 1928, p. 279; "How to Strengthen Schools," 1925, p. 3.

18. Diner, 1983, p. 96; Klaczynca, 1976; Bayor, 1988, pp. 26–29; Weisz, 1968, p. 83; Markowitz, 1993, pp. 20–21.

19. McGuffey, 1928, pp. 280–281; Moffett, 1929, pp. 6–7, 21; Hollis, 1929.

20. Morris, 1929, p. 2, W. H. Young, 1919, p. 375, Pulliam, 1930, Reese, 1928. For general discussions of this trend in educational research, see Knight, 1922, and S. Cohen, 1983.

21. Hoover quoted in Marsh, 1928, p. x; "Teachers Contract, 1923" quoted in Apple, 1988, p. 73.

22. "McAndrew on Clothing," 1925; "'Giddy' Teachers Not Wanted," 1922; New York Training School for Teachers, 1922; Bagley, 1922.

23. Board of Education of the City of New York, 1928.

24. "Men Teachers Needed," 1921; "How to Get Men Teachers," 1921. The "woman peril" in teaching was well noted by critics prior to World War I. See Ayres, 1911; Bardeen, 1912.

25. "Men Teachers and Shortage," 1927; High School Teachers' Association, 1921; "Agencies Report Surplus Women Teachers," 1926; Graebner, 1980, p. 101.

26. Rury, 1989; Steedman, 1985; Rousmaniere, 1994. Beecher quoted in Hoffman, 1981, p. 10.

27. Maltz, 1926.

28. Brody, 1928, p. 62; Tenenbaum, 1949; Addams, 1902, p. 196.

29. C. Cusumano (personal communication, 29 September 1990); I. Ross (personal communication, 5 October 1989); Markowitz, 1993; Cowan & Cowan, 1989, p. 98.

30. Yezierska, 1975, pp. 269–270.

31. Dublin, 1916; Mason, 1931.

32. Teacher-Training Institutions Should Recruit Their Quotas from the Nation's Most Promising Youth," 1926.

33. Markowitz, 1993, pp. 75–92.

34. School Survey Committee, 1924, p. 843.

35. Ware, 1965, pp. 67–68, 210, 214–215; M. L. Muir (personal communication, 2 November 1989).

36. A. Marsh (personal communication, 4 January 1991); I. Ross (personal communication, 5 October 1989).

37. Delany & Delany, 1993, pp. 168–170.

38. Berrol, 1967, pp. 52–53; Moore, 1981, pp. 96, 105–115; Gerwitz, 1981; Weinberg, 1977, pp. 73–74; Ment, 1983, p. 93; Cordasco, 1975, p. xii; Covello, 1958, p. 130.

39. Fitzpatrick v. Board of Education, 1910; Appeal of Rose Davidson et al., 1918; Markowitz, 1993, p. 87.

40. Citizens' Committee on Teachers' Salaries, 1927, p. 226; Goodsell, 1929, p. 8. For literature on the history of gender stratification within teaching, see Tyack & Strober, 1981; Strober & Best, 1979.

41. In the Matter of the Petition of Lillian Teece, 1922; In the Matter of the Appeal of Therese E. Simar, 1925.

42. Markowitz, 1993, pp. 132–150; Broom, 1929; Chambers, 1929; McGinnis, 1931.

43. Pine, 1977; A. Marsh (personal communication, 4 January 1991).

44. Richardson, 1928, p. 115; I. McNab (personal communication, 25 October 1989).

45. Connolly, 1919. Still, the 1920s marked the height of women's positions in school administration: 55% of the nation's school principals were women, the highest percentage of women administrators in the nation's history. Indeed, for women school administrators, as for women undergraduate and graduate students, women professors, and women college presidents, the early 1920s was a "golden age" that marked the high point of women's professional advancement in the education profession. See Tyack & Strober, 1981. In contrast, in the 1980s, only 20% of school principals were women. See Apple, 1989, p. 33.

46. M. Jamer (personal communication, 18 November 1989).

47. Citizen's Committee on Teachers' Salaries, 1927, p. 78. Cott, 1987, p. 130; I. Ross (personal communication, 12 October 1989).

48. M. Jamer (personal communication, 18 November 1989).

49. I. Ross (personal communication, 12 October 1989); I. McNab (personal communication, 25 October 1989); L. Skidmore (personal communication, 22 November 1989); M. Jamer (personal communication, 18 November 1989); M. L.

Muir (personal communication, 2 November 1989); A. Marsh (personal communication, 4 January 1991). See Markowitz, 1993, ch. 9, for an examination of anti-Semitism in the hiring of New York City teachers in the 1930s.

50. Higham, 1973, pp. 277–286; Pierce, 1926; Krug, 1972, pp. 9–17; Linville quoted in Murphy, 1990, p. 96.

51. Quoted in Brumberg, 1986, pp. 137–138; "Report of the Legal Advisory Committee," 1926; "Report of the Special Committee on the Assignment of Teachers on Jewish Holidays," 1929–30; Moore, 1981, p. 101; I. Ross & E. Padow (personal communication, 26 October 1989).

52. Mabee, 1979; Nifenecker, 1936, p. 127; J. W. Johnson, 1940, p. 26; Bowles, 1923.

53. Osofsky, 1966, pp. 81–104, 135–149; Ment, 1983, pp. 75–76.

54. S. Cousins (personal communication, 25 November 1989).

55. I. Ross (personal communication, 5 October 1989).

56. McDougald, 1925, p. 691.

CHAPTER 3

1. Ennis, 1918, p. 14.

2. Apple, 1989, pp. 41–45; Larson, 1980; Lawn & Ozga, 1981.

3. E. W. Stevens, 1972; Kliebard, 1987, pp. 111–115, 156–179; Franklin, 1986, pp. 83–118; Earle, 1928; Nasaw, 1985.

4. Shulman, 1938, pp. 85–87; Addams quoted in Lagemann, 1985, p. 136.

5. Krug, 1969, p. 388; Jenness, 1990, pp. 76–102; Boynton, 1917, pp. 95–97; Monro, 1916, Brumberg, 1990, Osgood, 1916.

6. Rosenthal & Bybee, 1987; Pauly, 1991.

7. Stanic, 1986; Breckenridge, 1921a, 1921b; J. K. Smith, 1912, pp. 385–494; Koch, 1917.

8. Grise, 1925; Magoffin & Henry, 1928/1932.

9. Krug, 1972, p. 105.

10. Quoted in Averill, 1917, p. 54

11. Chayer, 1937; Regan, 1974, pp. 24–60; Brooks, 1925; E. F. Brown, 1916.

12. Crampton, 1917, p. 11; Armstrong, 1921.

13. Board of Education of the City of New York, 1930, p. 17.

14. Imbar, 1984; D. Tyack & Hansot, 1990, pp. 220–227; Storey, Small, & Salisbury, 1922, pp. 5–10, 32; Spring, 1974; Jable, 1979.

15. McLure, 1924; Cole et al., 1931; Berkowitz, 1919.

16. S. Cohen, 1983, pp. 130–135.

17. Oppenheimer, 1924.

18. Tyack & Berkowitz, 1977; "Variation in School Attendance," 1922; Conklin, 1927, p. 96.

19. M. D. Gordon & Seasholes, 1930, pp. 8–12.

20. Cox, 1927, p. 48.

21. Buchholz, 1931, p. 115.

22. Board of Education of the City of New York, 1948, pp. 88–95.

23. Deffenbaugh, 1925; Tropea, 1987; Chapman, 1981.

24. Franklin, 1994; Raftery, 1988. For contemporary critiques of IQ tests by teachers, see Frank, 1923; Zinman, 1923; Carothers, 1924.

25. Carothers, 1923, p. 15; Covello, 1958, pp. 149–151.

26. C. Cusumano (personal communication, 29 September 1990); E. Gottlieb (personal communication, 8 October 1990); A. Marsh (personal communication, 4 January 1991).

27. E. Gottlieb (personal communication, 19 October 1990).

28. A. Marsh (personal communication, 4 January 1991).

29. Dent, 1930; Ballou, 1929.

30. School Survey Committee, 1924, pp. 1433–1438.

31. Cuban, 1993; Zilversmit, 1993.

32. Loftus, 1928, p. 255; Proctor & Brown, 1928, pp. 171–173.

33. R. Stevens, 1912; Armstrong, 1920; School Survey Committee, 1924, pp. 840–857.

34. School Survey Committee, 1924, p. 1268.

35. Armstrong, 1922; School Survey Committee, 1924, pp. 1368–1370.

36. Chicago Teachers Federation, 1921a, 1921b, 1930; Brooklyn Teachers Association, 1926, p. 11.

37. Owen, 1931.

38. Cowing, 1923; Phillips, 1926–27; Ennis, 1918.

39. A. Marsh (personal communication, 4 January 1991).

40. School Library Inventory Statistics, 1926–33; Tebbel, 1988; Batchelder, 1988; Jones, 1929.

41. Hyde, 1920; Armstrong, 1920; O'Malley, 1990, pp. 230–231; School Survey Committee, 1924, pp. 1203–1238; Hochheimer, 1926; Courtney, 1927.

42. Ballou, 1929; Dent, 1929.

43. Lefkowitz, 1929.

44. Jablonower, 1965.

45. Franklin, 1985; Hill, 1919, pp. 8–9.

46. Quoted in Beale, 1936, p. 74.

CHAPTER 4

1. S. M. Johnson, 1990, p. 1; Markus, 1993; Rousmaniere, 1996.

2. Maller, 1938.

3. Cutler, 1989, p. 8; Turner, 1987, pp. 117, 124; Rider, 1924, p. 323; Salwen, 1989, p. 88; Brumberg, 1986, p. 133.

4. Raymond, 1931, pp. 34–35; Sinclair, 1924, pp. 63–64; "What Women Investigators Found in Old City School Buildings," 1921; West of Central Park Association, 1937.

5. "Survey of Group of School Buildings by Outside Organizations," 1925, p. 868; Duffy, 1979; "Report on Construction and Maintenance," 1924, p. 16; Berkowitz, 1919.

6. "New School Buildings and Sites," 1926, pp. 19, 20; "Report on Construc-

tion and Maintenance," 1924, p. 11; Gompert, 1924; Board of Education of the City of New York, 1948, pp. 13, 46, 67, 81; Nifenecker, 1936, p. 65.

7. Anderson & Fowlkes, 1927; Newhouse, 1989, p. 28; Cutler, 1989.

8. Armstrong, 1921.

9. Fearon, 1928, p. 76; Gardner, 1921, p. 404; School Survey Committee, 1924, pp. 1318–1322, 1532.

10. "Report of Visit to P. S. 90," 1930 ("There was nothing, tho"); De Lima, 1924, p. 19 ("to call forth the slightest").

11. Gardner, 1921, p. 405; Dublin, 1916; Vaughan, 1928.

12. Hermalyn, 1985, p. 102; School Survey Committee, 1924, pp. 348–349; Raymond, 1931, p. 38; Sinclair, 1924, pp. 64–65.

13. "Help-Your-Own-School Suggestions," 1914, p. 14.

14. M. L. Muir (personal communication, 2 November 1989).

15. C. Cusumano (personal communication, 29 September 1990).

16. Harrison & Dobbin, 1931, p. 56; Galvin & Walker, 1929; McKown, 1930.

17. United Parents Association, 1929; Kittredge, 1926, p. 503; "Raps Lunchrooms in Public Schools," 1921.

18. "School Rest Rooms," 1925; Harrison & Dobbin, 1931, pp. 75, 160; Kessler-Harris, 1982, p. 185; School Survey Committee, 1924, p. 1367.

19. Teachers' Rest Room, 1922.

20. "Questions and Suggestions on the Physical Conditions of the Public Schools," n.d.

21. I. McNab (personal communication, 25 October 1989).

22. M. Jamer (personal communication, 18 November 1989).

23. McLure, 1924, pp. 2 13; School Survey Committee, 1924, p. 317.

24. I. Ross (personal communication, 12 October 1989).

25. Gardner, 1921; C. H. Sampson, 1922; "Angelo Patri Points Out Evils of Over-Crowding," 1922; "Says Big Classes Fordize Schools," 1929; "Brooklyn Overcrowded Schools," 1921; "High School Teachers to Protest," 1921; "Economy Plan Stands," 1921.

26. Chicago Teachers Federation, 1924.

27. Stevenson, 1923; Engelhardt, 1929, p. 162.

28. Case of Ida Calhoun, 1924.

29. A. Marsh (personal communication, 7 January 1991).

30. R. Cohen & Mohl, 1979; Ravitch, 1988, pp. 195–230.

31. Correspondence to Mrs. Hanson and Mr. Collette, 1924.

32. *Journal of the Board of Education of the City of New York,* 1922, pp. 2025–2031.

33. M. Jamer (personal communication, 18 November 1989).

34. School Survey Committee, 1924, pp. 1363, 1392–1396, 1579.

35. Quance, 1926, pp. 12 13.

36. I. McNab (personal communication, 25 October 1989).

37. I. McNab (personal communication, 25 October 1989).

38. Chicago Teachers Federation, 1925.

39. M. Jamer (personal communication, 18 November 1989).

40. R. Stern (personal communication, 31 October 1989).
41. Julia Richman High School, 1913–24, p. 51.
42. Julia Richman High School, 1913–24, p. 50.
43. Julia Richman High School, 1913–24, p. 131.
44. Julia Richman High School, 1913–24, p. 74.
45. Lepetes, 1919; School Survey Committee, 1924, p. 1576.

CHAPTER 5

1. "The Super-Vision Demanded in Supervision," 1928.
2. Apple, 1989; Densmore, 1987; Altenbaugh, 1987.
3. This reevaluation of deskilling and the "proletarianization" of teachers is best articulated in Ozga & Lawn, 1988. See also Taggart, 1995.
4. Braverman, 1974; Edwards, 1979.
5. Callahan, 1970, pp. 221–243. See also Eaton, 1990; Berman, 1983.
6. Quoted in Kliebard, 1987, p. 103; Taylor, 1912; Callahan, 1970, pp. 103–104; Welty, 1930; "The Chicago Schools," 1927, p. 362.
7. Courtis, 1928; Ettinger, 1921.
8. Lefkowitz, 1925; New York City Board of Education, 1928.
9. Markowitz, 1993, p. 95; "Board of Superintendents Recommends That Teachers' Tardiness be Recorded," 1922; Belding, 1928; "Public Address Systems," 1928–29, p. 263.
10. Bacon, 1928; Mossman, 1929; Bobbitt, 1924, pp. 13–14.
11. Temple, 1928; Gist & King, 1922; Hart, 1929.
12. School Survey Committee, 1924, pp. 840–978; "Twenty-Eighth Annual Report of the Superintendent of Schools, 1925–26," p. 49.
13. McClure, 1921; Davis, 1921; Cubberley, 1923.
14. "School Red Tape Repels Teachers," 1920; "Why Teachers Leave School," 1921; Bell, 1924, p. 13; "Confessions of a Teacher," 1920a; Holway, 1930, pp. 1–5.
15. "Report of Visit to P. S. 90," 1930.
16. Cook, 1923; Koons, 1920; Reed, 1927.
17. Armstrong, 1922.
18. A. Goldin (personal communication, 7 December 1989).
19. Armstrong, 1922.
20. "Confessions of a Teacher," 1920a.
21. Patri, n.d., p. 8.
22. I. Ross (personal communication, 5 October 1989); L. Skidmore (personal communication, 22 November 1989).
23. I. Ross (personal communication, 26 October 1989).
24. M. Jamer (personal communication, 18 November 1989).
25. S. Cousins (personal communication, 25 November 1989).
26. "Confessions of a Teacher," 1920b. See also Myra Kelly's turn-of-the-century description of teachers' warning signals to one another upon the visit of a particularly harsh superintendent in Hoffman, 1981, pp. 249–254.

27. D. Meyer (personal communication, 14 August 1990).

28. Scott, 1923.

29. M. L. Muir (personal communication, 2 November 1989); I. Ross (personal communication, 5 October 1989).

30. A. Goldin (personal communication, 7 December 1989).

31. I. McNab (personal communication, 25 October 1989).

32. Branson, 1930; Frazier, 1924.

33. Mossman, 1924, p. 28.

34. E. Gottlieb (personal communication, 19 October 1990).

35. Patri, n.d., p. 8.

36. I. Ross (personal communication, 5 October 1989).

37. "A Rebel Song," 1924.

38. School Survey Committee, 1924, p. 1405; I. McNab (personal communication, 25 October 1989).

39. C. Cusumano (personal communication, 29 September 1990).

40. I. McNab (personal communication, 25 October 1989).

41. R. Stern (personal communication, 31 October 1989).

42. "Two Stormy Years," 1916–1918; Cowan & Cowan, 1989, p. 242; D. Meyer (personal communication, 14 August 1990); E. Gottlieb (personal communication, 19 October 1990).

43. School Survey Committee, 1924, p. 1017.

44. Beale, 1936, p. 589.

45. School Survey Committee, 1924, pp. 1398–1416; Department of Classroom Teachers, 1926, p. 39.

46. School Survey Committee, 1924, p. 1403.

47. "Teacher and Clerk, Too," 1927.

48. Saltzberg, 1925. A poem written by a teacher in 1880 (quoted in Hoffman, 1981, p. 255) also referred to a teacher's death by too much paperwork: "She slept, she dreamed; it seemed she had died. / And her spirit went to Hades, / And they met her there with a questions fair, / 'State what the per cent of your grade is.'"

49. School Survey Committee, 1924, p. 1402.

50. Parsons, 1920; "Confessions of a Teacher," 1920a.

CHAPTER 6

1. De Lima, 1924, p. 19.

2. Cuban, 1993; Zilversmit, 1993; Finkelstein, 1989.

3. Maller, 1938; Nifenecker, 1936, p. 188; Conklin, 1929.

4. Nifenecker, 1936, pp. 190–192; Felt, 1965.

5. Brenzel, Roberts-Gersch, & Wittner, 1985; Earle, 1928, p. 332; Landesman, 1969, p. 156 ("traditional Jewish passion"); "Autobiography of a 16 Year Old Student," 1936 ("boys of all ages"); Nasaw, 1985, p. 26 ("school was all wrong").

6. Shulman, 1938, p. 71; Earle, 1928, p. 331; Brumberg, 1986, pp. 207–212; Thrasher, 1928.

7. Brumberg, 1986, p. 132; Cowan & Cowan, 1989, pp. 100–101; Mabee, 1979, pp. 249–250; Conklin, 1929, pp. 271–272.

8. Tropea, 1987; Franklin, 1994; Perlmann, 1985; Board of Education of the City of New York, 1922, p. 9; Brooklyn Teachers' Association, 1922, p. 20.

9. Dresslar, 1907; Harris, 1927, pp. 226–227, 249–274; Hiner, 1979, p. 244; Rich, 1924.

10. "Pupils Use Tiny Glass Bombs to Startle Teachers," 1922; "Four School-boys Held for Theft," 1921; "Fight and Death at Erasmus Hall," 1922; "Cry of 'Black Hand' Brings School Riot," 1926; Cowan & Cowan, 1989, pp. 100–101; "Play or Death?" 1926.

11. I. McNab (personal communication, 25 October 1989).

12. Yezierska, 1975, pp. 271–272.

13. M. Muir (personal communication, 2 November 1989).

14. I. Ross (personal communication, 12 October 1989).

15. D. Meyer (personal communication, 14 August 1990).

16. D. Meyer (personal communication, 14 August 1990).

17. Otis, 1922.

18. Mabee, 1979, p. 248; Ment, 1983, p. 71; Osofsky, 1966, pp. 17–34; Homel, 1984, pp. 190–191; Chivers & Bickford, 1924, p. 149.

19. Ment, 1983, pp. 92–93; Mabee, 1979, pp. 248–249; Chivers & Bickford, 1924, p. 151; Fauset, 1989, p. 40.

20. Waller, 1932, p. 195; Waller, 1970, pp. 233–245; Hansot, 1989.

21. Bourne, 1914, p. 23.

22. Wickman, 1928; Shulman, 1930; Cowan & Cowan, 1989, pp. 87–88; Brumberg, 1986, pp. 125–126.

23. Cowan & Cowan, 1989, p. 87.

24. A. Marsh (personal communication, 4 January 1991).

25. M. Jamer (personal communication, 18 November 1989).

26. I. Ross (personal communication, 12 October 1989); D. Meyer (personal communication, 14 August 1990).

27. I. McNab (personal communication, 25 October 1989).

28. Bolmeier, 1933; Falk, 1941, p. 2; "To Fine Mrs McQuirk?" 1921; "Acquits Brooklyn Teacher," 1927; Case of Mr. Switzer Smith, 1921; "Matter of Streamer," 1915; "Matter of Zeiner," 1922.

29. "Teachers Whose Services Have Been Discontinued," 1926; Craig, 1929; Loyd, 1930.

30. Bardeen, 1912, p. 27; "America 'Feminine,' Prof. Rogers Says," 1929; Dublin, 1916.

31. Rockwell, 1922; Barnhart, 1929.

32. D. Meyer (personal communication, 14 August 1990).

33. D. Meyer (personal communication, 14 August 1990).

34. I. Ross (personal communication, 12 October 1989); D. Meyer (personal communication, 14 August 1990); L. Skidmore (personal communication, 22 November 1989); Cowan & Cowan, 1989, p. 87.

35. I. McNab (personal communication, 25 October 1989).

36. L. Skidmore (personal communication, 22 November 1989).

37. I. Ross (personal communication, 12 October 1989); I. McNab (personal communication, 25 October 1989).

38. Bourne, 1914.

39. Bourne, 1914, p. 23; De Lima, 1924, p. 20.

40. Simon, 1982; quoted in Brumberg, 1986, p. 128.

41. McCullough, 1928.

42. Hastings, 1927.

43. Henderson, 1924a, p. 340; Collette, 1925.

44. H. Sampson, 1926; M. Brown, 1925, p. 486.

45. Henderson, 1924b.

46. A. Marsh (personal communication, 4 January 1991).

47. S. Cousins (personal communication, 25 November 1989).

48. Hodgen, 1959, pp. 131–132.

49. "School Heads Seek to Cut Waste Time," 1925; Armstrong, 1922.

50. O'Shea, 1924–25, pp. 41–42.

51. L. Gordon, 1988, pp. 177–181.

52. "Miss Zipfel's Bill Vetoed," 1921; "Miss Zipfel Sues the State," 1921.

EPILOGUE

1. Kaufman, 1964/1991, p. xv.

2. Taggart, 1995. For some of the few school reform initiatives that are teacher-driven, see Meier, 1995; Wood, 1992.

3. Carlson, 1992; Goldschmidt & Stuart, 1986.

References

Note: Archival collections cited include the following: Chicago Historical Society, Chicago (Chicago Teachers Federation papers); Walter P. Reuther Library [Reuther Library], Wayne State University Archives of Labor and Urban Affairs, Detroit (American Federation of Teachers papers, Henry Linville papers, Joseph Jablonower papers, Selma Borchardt papers, St. Paul Federation of Teachers collection); Milbank Memorial Library Special Collections, Teachers College, Columbia University, New York (Department of Nursing Education, Teachers College, department files; United Parents Association papers; Archives of the Board of Education of the City of New York [BOE]); Tamiment Institute Library, The Robert F. Wagner Labor Archives [Wagner Archives], New York University, New York (United Federation of Teachers papers); Library of Congress, Washington, D.C. (Angelo Patri papers).

Acquits Brooklyn teacher. (1927, November 3). *New York Times*, p. 3.

Addams, J. (1902). *Democracy and social ethics*. New York: Macmillan.

Agencies report surplus women teachers. (1926, October 31). *New York Times*, p. 15.

Alexander, C. (1910). *Some present aspects of the work of teachers' voluntary associations in the United States*. New York: Teachers College Press.

Allen, F. L. (1931). *Only yesterday: An informal history of the 1920s*. New York: Harper & Brothers.

Altenbaugh, R. J. (1992). *The teachers' voice: A social history of teaching in twentieth century America*. Bristol, PA: Falmer.

America "Feminine," Prof. Rogers says. (1929, September 9). *New York Times*, pp. 1, 11.

Anderson, C. J., & Fowlkes, J. G. (1927). *Study of budgeting and allotment of school supplies*. Madison: University of Wisconsin Press.

Angelo Patri points out evils of over-crowding. (1922, May 11). *School, 33*, 621.

Appeal of Rose Davidson et al. (1918). Case No. 434, *Department Reports of the State of New York, 17*.

Apple, M. (1989). *Teachers and texts: A political economy of class and gender relations in education*. New York: Routledge.

Armstrong, M. G. (1920, November 20). "Movies" coming into their own in New York schools. *New York Evening Post,* p. 12.

Armstrong, M. G. (1921, April 23). Community needs role in new school buildings. *New York Evening Post,* p. 13.

Armstrong, M. G. (1922, January 21). Why aren't more teachers really happy? *New York Evening Post,* p. 11.

Aspinwall, W. B. (1921). The value of student teaching in a teacher-training course. *Educational Administration and Supervision, 7,* 103–110.

Autobiography of a 16 year old student. (1936). Angelo Patri Papers, Box 88, Library of Congress.

Averill, L. A. (1917). The present status of school health work in the 100 largest cities of the United States. *The American Journal of School Hygiene, 1,* 53–62.

Ayres, L. P. (1911). What educators think about the need for employing men teachers in our public schools. *Journal of Educational Psychology, 2,* 89–93.

Bacon, F. L. (1928). Supervision in the secondary school from the viewpoint of the principal. *Addresses and Proceedings of the National Education Association,* 718–723.

Bagley, W. C. (1922). Preparing teachers for the urban service. *Educational Administration and Supervision, 8,* 398–401.

Ballou, F. W. (1929, June 26). Correspondence to the board of education of the District of Columbia. Selma Borchardt papers, Box 134, Folder 14, Reuther Library.

Bardeen, C. W. (1912). The monopolizing woman teacher. *Educational Review, 43,* 17–40.

Barker, J., & Downing, H. (1980). Word processing and transformation of the patriarchal relations of control in the office. *Capital and Class, 10,* 64–97.

Barnhart, N. G. (1929). Is corporal punishment still necessary? *Journal of Education, 110,* 546–547.

Bashaw, C. T. (1986). Ella Flagg Young and her relationship to the cult of efficiency. *Educational Theory, 36,* 363–374.

Batchelder, M. (1988). The leadership network in children's librarianship: A remembrance. In S. A. Jagusch (Ed.), *Stepping away from tradition: Children's books of the twenties and thirties* (pp. 71–120). Washington, DC: Library of Congress.

Bayor, R. H. (1988). *Neighbors in conflict: The Irish, Germans, Jews, and Italians of New York City, 1929–1941.* Chicago: University of Illinois Press.

Beale, H. K. (1936). *Are American teachers free?* New York: Scribners.

Belding, A. W. (1928). Aids to the principal. *Journal of Education, 107,* 634.

Bell, A. D. (1924). The grade school principal as seen from the teacher's desk. *Popular Education, 42,* 12–13, 45.

Ben-Peretz, M. (1995). *Learning from experience: Memory and the teacher's account of teaching.* Albany: State University of New York Press.

Benson, S. P. (1988). *Counter cultures: Saleswomen, managers, and customers in American department stores, 1890–1940.* Chicago: University of Illinois Press.

Berkowitz, J. H. (1919). *The eyesight of school children (Bulletin No. 65).* Washington, DC: U.S. Bureau of Education.

Berman, B. (1983). Business efficiency, American schooling, and the public school superintendency: A reconsideration of the Callahan thesis. *History of Education Quarterly, 23,* 297–321.

Berrol, S. (1967). *Immigrants at school: New York City, 1898–1914.* Unpublished doctoral dissertation, City University of New York, New York.

Berrol, S. (1976). Education and economic mobility: The Jewish experience in New York City, 1880–1920. *American Jewish Historical Quarterly, 65,* 257–271.

Board of Education of the City of New York. (1922). *Syllabus for high schools: English.*

Board of Education of the City of New York. (1928). *The Teacher's Handbook.* New York: Author.

Board of Education of the City of New York. (1930). *Course of study in health education for elementary schools, grades 1A–8B: Part I. Physiology, personal and community hygiene.* New York: Author.

Board of Education of the City of New York. (1948). *The first fifty years: 1898–1948.* New York: Author.

Board of superintendents recommends that teachers' tardiness be recorded. (1922, December 22). *School, 33,* 289.

Bobbitt, F. (1924). Functions of the high school principal in curriculum-making. *National Association of Secondary School Principals, Eighth Yearbook.*

Bogan, W. J. (1919). The value of teachers' council. *Addresses and Proceedings of the National Education Association,* 387–389.

Bolmeier, E. C. (1933). The law governing the corporal punishment of pupils. *Elementary School Journal, 33,* 527–536.

Bourne, R. (1914). In a schoolroom. *The New Republic, 7,* 23–24.

Bowles, F. D. (1923). Opportunities for educated colored women. *Opportunity, 1,* 8–10.

Boynton, G. E. (1917). The use of current literature. *The History Teachers' Magazine, 7,* 95–99.

Branson, L. (1930). Behind school doors. *The Union Teacher, 7,* 7–8.

Braverman, H. (1974). *Labor and monopoly capital: The degradation of work in the twentieth century.* New York: Monthly Review Press.

Breckenridge, W. (1921a). The slide rule as a subject of regular class instruction in mathematics. *The Mathematics Teacher, 14,* 342–343.

Breckenridge, W. (1921b). Mathematics in Stuyvesant High School. *The Mathematics Teacher, 14,* 86.

Breckinridge, S. (1972). *Women in the twentieth century: A study of their political, social and economic activities.* New York: Arno Press.

Brenzel, B., Roberts-Gersch, C., & Wittner, J. (1985). Becoming social: School girls and their culture between the two world wars. *Journal of Early Adolescence, 5,* 479–488.

Brody, C. (1928). A New York childhood. *American Mercury, 14,* 57–66.

Brooklyn Overcrowded Schools. (1921, February 17). *School, 32,* 429.

Brooklyn Teachers' Association. Forty-sixth annual report. (1919–20).

Brooklyn Teachers' Association. Forty-eighth annual report. (1922).

Brooklyn Teachers' Association. Fifty second annual report. (1926).

Brooks, V. H. (1925). The place of the school nurse in the school health program. *Public Health Nurse, 17,* 458.

Broom, M. E. (1929). Married teachers. *High School Teacher, 5,* 228.

Brown, D. M. (1987). *Setting a course: American women in the 1920s.* Boston: Twayne.

Brown, E. F. (1916). The health supervision of the school children of New York City. Teachers College Department of Nursing Education Files, 1910–58, Box 1, Folder "Material on School Nursing." Milbank Memorial Library.

Brown, M. (1925). Rondeau in a classroom. *The English Journal, 14,* 486.

Brumberg, S. F. (1986). *Going to America, going to school: The Jewish immigrant public school encounter in turn-of-the century New York City.* New York: Praeger.

Brumberg, S. F. (1990). New York City schools march off to war: The nature and extent of participation of the city schools in the Great War, April 1917–June 1918. *Urban Education, 24,* 440–475.

Buchholz, H. E. (1931). *Fads and fallacies in education.* New York: Macmillan.

Callahan, R. E. (1970). *Education and the cult of efficiency.* Chicago: University of Chicago Press.

Carlson, D. (1992). *Teachers and crisis: Urban school reform and teachers' work culture.* New York: Routledge.

Carothers, F. E. (1923). The use of psychological tests at Washington Irving High School. *Ungraded, 9,* 15–18.

Carothers, F. E. (1924). Elementary school group classification of pupils versus intelligence tests classification. *High Points, 6,* 9–12.

Carter, P. (1992). Becoming the "new woman": The equal rights campaigns of New York City schoolteachers, 1900–1920. In R. J. Altenbaugh (Ed.), *The teacher's voice: A social history of teaching in twentieth century America* (pp. 40–58). Bristol, PA: Falmer.

Carter, P. (1985). *A coalition between women teachers and the feminist movement in New York City, 1900–1920.* Unpublished doctoral dissertation, University of Cincinnati.

Carter, S. B. (1989). Incentives and rewards to teaching. In D. Warren (Ed.), *American teachers: Histories of a profession at work* (pp. 49–62). New York: Macmillan.

Carter, S. B., & Prus, M. (1982). The labor market and the American high school girl 1890–1928. *Journal of Economic History, 49,* 163–171.

Carter, S. B., & Savoca, E. (1992). The "teaching procession"? Another look at teacher tenure, 1845–1925. *Explorations in Economic History, 29,* 401–416.

Case against efficiency, The. (1916). *The American Teacher, 5,* 33.

Case of Ida Calhoun. (1924). Chicago Teachers Federation General Files, Box 52, Folder November–December. Chicago Historical Society.

Case of Mr. Switzer Smith. (1921). Case No. 670, *New York State Department Records, 26,* 36–39.

Chambers, M. M. (1929). A plea for married women teachers. *School and Society, 30,* 572.

Chapman, P. D. (1981). Schools as sorters: Testing and tracking in California, 1910–1925. *Journal of Social History, 14,* 701–717.

Chayer, M. E. (1937). *School nursing: A contribution to health education.* New York: Putnam.

Chicago schools, The. (1927). *School and Society, 26,* 361–362.

Chicago Teachers Federation. (1921a). Council group 30. Chicago Teachers Federation, General Files, Box 48, Folder August–October 1921. Chicago Historical Society.

Chicago Teachers Federation. (1921b). Council group 31. Chicago Teachers Federation, General Files, Box 48, Folder August–October 1921. Chicago Historical Society.

Chicago Teachers Federation. (1924, November 8). Regular meeting minutes, Chicago Teachers Federation General Files, Box 4. Chicago Historical Society.

Chicago Teachers Federation. (1925, February 14). Regular meeting minutes, Chicago Teachers Federation General Files, Box 5. Chicago Historical Society.

Chicago Teachers Federation. (1930, February 15). Regular meeting minutes, Chicago Teachers Federation General Files, Box 10. Chicago Historical Society.

Chivers W. R., & Bickford, M. E. (1924). Over-age Negro children. *Opportunity, 2,* 149–151.

Churchill, T. (1916). Report of the president of the board of education. In *The teachers' council of the Department of Education of the City of New York: Its history, purpose, organization, work.* New York: Board of Education.

Citizen's committee on teachers' salaries. (1927). *Teachers' Salaries in New York City.* New York: Teachers College Press.

Clifford, G. J. (1989). Man/woman/teacher: Gender, family and career in American educational history. In D. Warren (Ed.), *American teachers: Histories of a profession at work* (pp. 293–343). New York: Macmillan.

Coffman, L. D. (1911). *The social composition of the teaching population.* New York: Teachers College Press.

Cohen, R., & Mohl, R. (1979). *The paradox of progressive education: The Gary Plan and urban schooling.* Port Washington, NY: Kennikat Press.

Cohen, S. (1983). The mental hygiene movement, the development of personality and the school: The medicalization of American education. *History of Education Quarterly, 23,* 123–149.

Cole, R., Kimball, D. D., Lee, F. S., Palmer, G. T., Palmer, E. B., Thorndike, E. L., & Winslow, C. E. A. (1931). A study of ventilation and respiratory illnesses in New York City Schools: Comparison of window-gravity ventilation and of unit fan ventilation with varying air flow. *American Journal of Hygiene, 13,* 235–254.

Collette, E. (1925). Monotone. *The English Journal, 14,* 640.

Confessions of a teacher: "Psychology" and supervision. (1920a, November 20). *New York Evening Post,* p. 12.

Confessions of a teacher: The machinery of the schools. (1920b, November 13). *New York Evening Post,* p. 12.

Conklin, A. M. (1927). The school as a new tool. *Journal of Educational Sociology, 1,* 93–99.

Conklin, A. M. (1929). Children crying for the moon. *Journal of Educational Sociology, 5,* 263–277.

Connolly, L. (1919, March 8). Is there room at the top for women educators? *The Woman Citizen,* 840.

Cook, S. (1923). Teachers' idea of helpful supervision. *Educational Administration and Supervision, 9,* 554–557.

Cordasco, F. (Ed.). (1975). *The Italian community and its language in the United States: The annual reports of the Italian Teachers Association.* Totowa, NJ: Rowman & Littlefield.

Correspondence to Mrs. Hanson and Mr. Collette. (1924, November 3). American Federation of Teachers Collection, Series VI, Box 1, Folder "Chicago Women's Teachers Union, 1916–34." Reuther Library.

Cott, N. (1987). *The grounding of modern feminism.* New Haven, CT: Yale University Press.

Counts, G. (1922). *The selective character of American secondary education.* Chicago: University of Chicago Press.

Courtis, S. A. (1928). A philosophy of supervision. In J. F. Hosic (Ed.), *Educational supervision: A report of current views, investigations and practices* (pp. 249–258). New York: Teachers College Press.

Courtney, A. W. (1927). Films for schools. *The School Parent, 6,* 2–3.

Covello, L. (1958). *The heart is the teacher.* New York: McGraw-Hill.

Cowan, N., & Cowan, R. S. (1989). *Our parents' lives: The Americanization of Eastern European Jews.* New York: Basic Books.

Cowing, H. H. (1923). A teacher's time. *The School Review, 31,* 351–362.

Cox, P. W. L. (1927). Behavior adjustments and the junior high school curriculum. *The Journal of Educational Sociology, 1,* 37–48.

Coxe, W. W. (1931). *Study of high school teachers in New York State* (University of the State of New York Bulletin No. 964). Albany: University of the State of New York.

Craig, K. L. (1929). Is corporal punishment still necessary? *Journal of Education, 110,* 350.

Crampton, C. W. (1917). Cross section of the hygiene work of the Department of Physical Training, Bureau of Education, New York City. *The American Journal of School Hygiene, 1,* pp. 9–15.

Creighton, H. (1982). Tied by double apron strings: Female work culture and organization in a restaurant. *Insurgent Socialist, 11,* 59–64.

Cremin, L. (1964). *The transformation of the school: Progressivism in American education. 1876–1980.* New York: Vintage.

Crisis in education, The. (1920) *High Points 2,* 31–32.

Cry of "Black Hand" brings school riot. (1926, June 12). *New York Times,* p. 17.

Cuban, L. (1993). *How teachers taught: Constancy and change in American classrooms, 1890–1980* (2d ed.). New York: Teachers College Press.

Cubberley, E. P. (1923). *The principal and his school.* New York: Houghton Mifflin.

Cutler, W. W. (1989). Cathedral of culture: The schoolhouse in American educational thought and practice since 1820. *History of Education Quarterly, 29,* 1–40.

Davis, C. O. (1921). The duties of the high school principal. *School Review, 29,* 337–350.

Deffenbaugh, W. S. (1925). *Uses of intelligence and achievement tests in 215 cities* (City School Leaflet No. 20). Washington, DC: U.S. Bureau of Education.

Delany, S., & Delany, A. E., with Hearth, A. H. (1993). *Having our say: The Delany Sisters' first 100 years.* New York: Dell.

De Lima, A. (1924, November 12). Any school morning. *The New Republic, 10,* 19–20.

De Lima, A. (1926). *Our enemy, the child.* New York: The New Republic.

Densmore, K. (1987). Professionalism, proletarianization and teacher work. In T. S. Popkewitz (Ed.), *Critical studies in teacher education: Its folklore, theory and practice* (pp. 130–160). New York: Falmer.

Dent, M. C. (1929, June 19). Correspondence to Mr. B. A. Bowles. Selma Borchardt papers, Box 134, Folder 14. Reuther Library.

Dent, M. C. (1930, February 17). Correspondence to the board of education. Selma Borchardt papers, Box 134, Folder 14. Reuther Library.

Department of Classroom Teachers, National Education Association. (1926). *Yearbook.* Washington, DC: Author.

Derber, M. (1966). The idea of industrial democracy in America. *Labor History, 7,* 259–286.

Desmond, S. (1919, April 6). New York, the unimaginable. *The New York Times Magazine,* 7.

di Leonardo, M. (1985). Women's work, work culture, and consciousness. *Feminist Studies, 11,* 491–495.

Diner, H. R. (1983). *Erin's daughters in America.* Baltimore: Johns Hopkins University Press.

Doherty, R. E. (1979). Tempest on the Hudson: The struggle for "equal pay for equal work" in the New York City public schools, 1907–1911. *History of Education Quarterly, 19,* 413–434.

Douglas, A. (1995). *Terrible honesty: Mongrel Manhattan in the 1920s.* New York: Farrar, Straus & Giroux.

Dressler, F. B. (1907). The contribution of twenty five years of organized child study in America to educational theory and practice as applied to the grammar grades. *Addresses and Proceedings of the National Education Association,* 910–914.

Dublin, L. (1916). Physical disability of New York City School teachers. *School and Society, 4,* 564–569.

Duffy, J. (1979). School buildings and the health of American school children in the nineteenth century. In C. Rosenberg (Ed.), *Healing and history* (pp. 161–178). New York: Science History.

Dumenil, L. (1995). *The modern temper: American culture and society in the 1920s.* New York: Hill & Wang.

Earle, M. G. (1928). A study of the effects of neighborhood backgrounds. *Journal of Educational Sociology, 1,* 330–338.

Eaton, W. E. (Ed.). (1990). *Shaping the superintendency: A reexamination of Callahan and "the cult of efficiency."* New York: Teachers College Press.

Economy plan stands. (1921, March 17). *School, 32,* 494.

Edwards, R. (1979). *Contested terrain: The transformation of the workplace in the twentieth century.* New York: Basic Books.

Engelhardt, N. L. (1929). The effective utilization of the high school plant. *Proceedings of the Annual Meeting of the National Association of Secondary School Principals.*

Ennis, I. (1918). What the public owes the teacher. In *Forty-fourth annual report of the Brooklyn Teachers Association,* pp. 13–18.

Ettinger, W. (1919). Address to district superintendents. *High Points, 1,* 1–15.

Ettinger, W. (1921). *Economy in school administration* (Annual Report of the Superintendent of Schools, New York City Board of Education). New York: Board of Education.

Fahey, S. (1919). Some causes of the present decline of teaching as a profession. *Addresses and proceedings of the National Education Association,* 383–387.

Falk, H. A. (1941). *Corporal punishment.* New York: Teachers College Press.

Fass, P. S. (1977). *The damned and the beautiful: American youth in the 1920s.* New York: Oxford University Press.

Fauset, J. R. (1989). *There is confusion.* Boston: Northeastern University Press.

Fearon, J. E. (1928). What teachers want in school buildings. *American School Board Journal, 76,* 76, 165.

Felt, J. P. (1965). *Hostage of fortune: Child labor reform in New York State.* Syracuse, NY: Syracuse University Press.

Fight and death at Erasmus Hall. (1922, January 11). *School, 33,* 19.

Finkelstein, B. (1989). *Governing the young: Teacher behavior in popular primary schools in nineteenth-century United States.* New York: Falmer.

Fitzpatrick v. Board of Education, 69 Miscellaneous Reports, New York 78 (1910).

Former teachers as government employees. (1921, April 15). *School Life, 6,* 5–6.

Four schoolboys held for theft. (1921, March 19). *New York Evening Post,* p. 18.

Frank, C. D. (1923). A ray of light let in by a study of first-term failures. *High Points, 5,* 6–7.

Franklin, B. M. (1985). The social efficiency movement and curriculum change, 1939–1976. In I. Goodson (Ed.), *Social histories of the secondary curriculum: Subjects for study* (pp. 239–268). London: Falmer.

Franklin, B. M. (1986). *Building the American curriculum: The school curriculum and the search for social control.* Philadelphia: Falmer.

Franklin, B. M. (1994). *From "backwardness" to "at risk": Childhood learning difficulties and the contradictions of school reform.* Albany: State University of New York Press.

Fraser, J. (1989). Agents of democracy: Urban elementary-school teachers and the conditions of teaching. In D. Warren (Ed.), *American teachers: Histories of a profession at work* (pp. 118–156). New York: Macmillan.

Frazier, B. W. (1924). The human factor in supervision. *American School Board Journal, 69,* 35.

Freeman, J., Lichtenstein, N., Brier, S., Bensman, D., Benson, S. P., Brundage, D, Eynon, B., Levine, B., & Palmer, B. (1992). *Who built America: Working people and the nation's economy, politics, culture, and society* (Vol. II). New York: Pantheon.

Galvin, E. H., & Walker, M. E. (1929). *Assemblies for junior and senior high schools.* New York: Professional and Technical Press.

Gardner, E. M. (1921). The school building in its reaction on the teacher's work. *Addresses and proceedings of the National Education Association,* pp. 404–406.

Gerwitz, M. (1981, May 18). Interviewed by David Ment, MG 70, Special Collections, Milbank Memorial Library, Teachers College, Columbia University.

Giddy teachers not wanted. (1922, March 2). *School, 33,* 461.

Gist, A. S., & King, W. A. (1922). The efficiency of the principalship from the standpoint of the teacher. *The Elementary School Journal, 23,* 120–126.

Goldschmidt, S. M., & Stuart, L. E. (1986). The extent and impact of educational policy bargaining. *Industrial and Labor Relations Review, 39,* 350–359.

Gompert, W. H. (1924). New York's colossal schoolhousing problem. *American School Board Journal, 69,* 51.

Goodlad, J. I. (1984). *A place called school: Prospects for the future.* New York: McGraw-Hill.

Goodsell, W. (1929). The educational opportunities of American women—Theoretical and actual. *Annals, 143,* 198–221.

Gordon, L. (1988). *Heroes of their own lives: The politics and history of family violence.* New York: Viking.

Gordon, M. D., & Seasholes, H. C. (1930). *The homeroom teacher.* Newark, NJ: Neighbor & Riggs.

Graebner, W. (1980). *A history of retirement: The meaning and function of an American institution, 1885–1978.* New Haven, CT: Yale University Press.

Graves, F. P. (1934). *Report of a study of New York City schools; Part II. Evaluation of achievement.* Albany: State University of New York Press.

Grise, F. C. (1925). *Content and method in high school Latin from the viewpoint of pupils and teachers.* Nashville, TN: George Peabody College for Teachers.

Gross, M. (1917). *Teachers' Council: Annual report of president and of recording secretary for the year 1917.* New York: Department of Education of the City of New York.

Gruenberg, B. (1912). Some economic obstacles to economic progress. *American Teacher, 1,* 90.

Haley, M. (1904). Why teachers should organize. *Addresses and proceedings of the National Education Association, 146,* 148–151.

Hammack, D. (1973). *Participation in major decisions in New York City 1890–1900: The creation of Greater New York and the centralization of the public school system.* Unpublished doctoral dissertation, Columbia University, New York.

Handwashing facilities in schools. (School Health Bureau, Monograph No. 3). (1928). New York: Metropolitan Life Insurance Co.

Harris, P. E. (1927). *Changing conceptions of school discipline.* New York: Macmillan.

Harrison, W. K., & Dobbin, C. E. (1931). *School buildings of today and tomorrow* New York: Architectural Book Publishing.

Hart, M. C. (1929). Supervision from the standpoint of the supervised. *School Review, 37,* 537–540.

Hastings, M. F. (1927). Examinations. *The English Journal, 16,* 463.

Help-your-own-school suggestions: Extracts from a field study of P. S. 188B Manhattan made at the request of principal Edward Mandel. (1914). New York: Bureau of Municipal Research.

Henderson, R. E. (1924a). Lecture period. *The English Journal, 13,* 340.

Henderson, R. E. (1924b). Teachering. *The English Journal, 13,* 583.

Hermalyn, G. (1985). *The creation of Morris High School, 1896–1904.* Unpublished doctoral dissertation, Teachers College, Columbia University, New York.

High School Teachers Association of New York City, The. (1921). *The high schools of New York City.* New York: Author.

High School Teachers' Association. (1921). *The high schools of New York City.* New York: Author.

High School Teachers to Protest. (1921, February 24). *School, 32,* 445.

Higham, J. (1973). *Strangers in the land: Patterns in American nativism, 1860–1925.* New York: Atheneum.

Hill, S. (1919). Defects of supervision and constructive suggestions thereon. *League of Teachers' Associations Bulletin, 4,* 4–11.

Hiner, N. R. (1979). Children's rights, corporal punishment, and child abuse, changing American attitudes, 1870–1920. *Bulletin of the Menniger Clinic, 43,* 233–248.

Hochheimer, R. (1926). Visual instruction: What is it? *The School Parent, 4,* 8–9.

Hodgen, M. D. (1959). *A high school in perspective: The characteristics of high school life on Staten Island, 1881–1926.* Unpublished doctoral dissertation, Teachers College, Columbia University, New York.

Hoffman, N. (1981). *Woman's "true" profession: Voices from the history of teaching.* Old Westbury, NY: Feminist Press.

Hollis, E. V. (1929). A personnel study of Teachers College students. *Journal of Educational Sociology, 4,* 320–329.

Holway, C. W. (1930). *How my principal could have helped me more as a classroom teacher.* Unpublished master's thesis, Teachers College, Columbia University, New York.

Homel, M. W. (1984). *Down from equality: Black Chicagoans and the public schools: 1920–41.* Chicago: University of Illinois Press.

Hooks, J. M. (1947). *Women's occupations through seven decades* (Women's Bureau Bulletin No. 218). Washington, DC: U.S. Department of Labor.

Horowitz, M. C., & Kaplan, L. (1959). *Jewish population in the New York Area, 1900–1975.* New York: Federation of Jewish Philanthropies.

How to get men teachers. (1921, May 12). *School, 32,* 630.

How to strengthen the schools. (1925). *Journal of the National Education Association, 14,* 3–4.

Hyde, G. M. (1920, July 17). Education motion pictures indorsed. *New York Evening Post,* p. 5.

Imbar, M. (1984). The First World War, sex education, and the American Social Hygiene Association's campaign against venereal disease. *Journal of Educational Administration and History, 16,* 47–56.

In the matter of the appeal of Therese E. Simar. (1925). Case No. 963. *Department Reports of the State of New York, 32,* 604–608.

In the matter of the petition of Lillian Teece. (1922). Case No. 745. *Department Reports of the State of New York, 27,* 652–656.

Jable, J. T. (1979). The Public School Athletic League of New York City: Organized athletics for city schoolchildren, 1903–1914. In W. M. Ladd & A. Lumpkin (Eds.), *Sport in American education: History and perspective* (pp. ix–18). Washington, DC: American Alliance for Health, Physical Education, Recreation and Dance.

Jablonower, J. (1965). Oral history. Oral History Research Office, Columbia University. Joseph Jablonower papers, Reuther Library.

Jenness, D. (1990). *Making sense of social studies.* New York: Macmillan.

Johnson, J. W. (1940). *Black Manhattan.* New York: Knopf.

Johnson, S. M. (1990). *Teachers at work: Achieving success in our schools.* New York: Basic Books.

Jones, O. M. (1929). Bad boys and the library hour. *Journal of Educational Sociology, 2,* 290–299.

Joseph, P. B. (1994). "The ideal teacher": Images of paragons in teacher education textbooks before 1940. In P. B. Joseph & G. E. Burnaford (Eds.), *Images of schoolteachers in twentieth-century America: Paragons, polarities, complexities* (pp. 258–282). New York: St. Martin's Press.

Journal of the Board of Education of the City of New York. (1922). New York: Board of Education of the City of New York.

Julia Richman High School. (1913–24). *The Blue Bird: 1913–24.* New York: Author.

Kaestle, C. (1973). *The evolution of an urban school system: New York City, 1750–1850.* Cambridge, MA: Harvard University Press.

Kanpol, B. (1988). Teacher work tasks as forms of resistance and accommodation to structural factors of schooling. *Urban Education, 23,* 173–187.

Kanter, R. M. (1977). *Men and women of the corporation.* New York: Basic Books.

Kaufman, B. (1991). *Up the down staircase.* New York: Harper. (Originally published 1964)

Kessler-Harris, A. (1982). *Out to work: A history of wage-earning women in the United States.* New York: Oxford University Press.

Klaczynca, B. (1976). Why women worked: A comparison of different groups: Philadelphia, 1910–30. *Labor History, 17,* 73–87.

Kliebard, H. (1987). *The struggle for the American curriculum: 1893–1958.* New York: Routledge & Kegan Paul.

Knight, F. B. (1922). *Qualities related to success in teaching.* New York: Teachers College Press.

Koch, E. H. (1917). Mathematical contests. *The Mathematics Teacher, 9,* 179–187.

Koons, C. (1920). View point of the teacher on supervisors. *Pennsylvania School Journal,* 419–451.

Krug, E. A. (1972). *The shaping of the American high school, 1920–1941.* Madison: University of Wisconsin Press.

Krug, E. A. (1969). *The shaping of the American high school: 1880–1920.* Madison: University of Wisconsin Press.

Lagemann, E. C. (Ed.). (1985). *Jane Addams on education.* New York: Teachers College Press.

Landesman, A. F. (1969). *Brownsville: The birth, development and passing of a Jewish community in New York.* New York: Block.

Larson, M. S. (1980). Proletarianization and educated labor. *Theory and Society, 9,* 131–175.

Lawn, M., & Ozga, J. (1981). The educational worker? A re-assessment of teachers. In L. Barton & S. Walker (Eds.), *Schools, teachers, and teaching* (pp. 45–64). New York: Falmer.

Lays mania for facts as bane of education. (1928, December 5). *New York Times,* p. 10.

Lefkowitz, A. (1924, February). The sword of intolerance. *The New York Teacher,* p. 2.

Lefkowitz, A. (1925). A study of the rating and the supervision of teachers in public school systems. BOE, Pamphlet Collection, Box 32. Milbank Memorial Library.

Lefkowitz, A. (1929). Dehumanizing education. *The Union Teacher, 7,* 2–3.

Lepetes, C. (1919, February 4). Correspondence to Henry Linville. Henry Linville Papers, Box 3, Folder Feb. 1–15, 1919. Reuther Library.

Linville, H. (1924, April). A plan for practical democracy. *The New York Teacher,* pp. 2–3.

Locke, L. L. (1914–15). Report on the swimming pool. *Brooklyn Teachers Association Forty-First Annual Report.*

Loftus, J. J. (1928). A practical revision of an elementary school curriculum. *Journal of Educational Sociology, 1,* 255–261.

Loyd, V. (1930). Corporal punishment. *School and Community, 16,* 78.

Mabee, C. (1979). *Black education in New York State.* Syracuse, NY: Syracuse University Press.

Magoffin, R. V. D., & Henry, M. Y. (1932). *Latin—First year.* New York: Silver Burdett. (Original work published 1928)

Maller, J. B. (1938). *School and community: Report of the regents' inquiry.* New York: McGraw-Hill.

Maltz, J. I. (1926). A tribute. *Brooklyn Teachers Association Fifty-Second Annual Report.* p. 20.

Markowitz, R. J. (1993). *My daughter, the teacher: Jewish teachers in New York City schools.* New Brunswick, NJ: Rutgers University Press.

Markus, T. (1993). *Buildings and power: Freedom and control in the origin of modern building types.* New York: Routledge.

Marsh, J. F. (1928). *The teacher outside the school.* New York: World Book.

Mason, F. V. (1931). A study of seven hundred maladjusted schoolteachers. *Mental Hygiene Magazine, 15,* 576–599.

Matter of Streamer. (1915). Case No. 291. *Department Reports of the State of New York, 6,* 611–615.

Matter of Zeiner. (1922). Case No. 747. *Department Reports of the State of New York, 27,* 682–683.

May, L. (1980). *Screening out the past: The birth of mass culture and the motion picture industry.* New York: Oxford University Press.

Mayman, J. E. (1917). Business and education. *The American Teacher, 6,* 82–86.

McAndrew on clothing. (1925, October). *The Indiana Teacher,* p. 20.

McAuliffe, W. J. (1920). *Teachers Council: Annual report of president and of recording secretary for the Year 1920.* New York: Department of Education of the City of New York.

McClure, W. (1921). The work outlined. *Bulletin of the Department of Elementary School Principals, 3,* 3–4.

McCullough, M. E. (1928). Teaching. *The English Journal, 17,* 53.

McDougald, E. J. (1925). The double task: The struggle of Negro women for race and sex emancipation. *Survey Graphic, 53,* 689–691.

McGinnis, W. C. (1931). The married woman teacher. *School Executive Magazine, 50,* 452.

McGuffey, V. (1928). Some elements in the cultural background of students in one of the New York City training schools for teachers. *Educational Administration and Supervision, 14,* 279–282.

McKown, H. C. (1930). *Assembly and auditorium activities.* New York: McMillan.

McLure, J. R. (1924). *The ventilation of school buildings.* New York: Teachers College Press.

McManis, J. T. (1916). *Ella Flagg Young and a half-century of the Chicago public schools.* Chicago: A. C. McClurg.

Meier, D. (1995). *The power of their ideas.* Boston: Beacon.

Melosh, B. (1982). *"The physician's hand": Work culture and conflict in American nursing.* Philadelphia: Temple University Press.

Memorandum submitted by various teachers associations of the City of New York in opposition to Senate Bill 481, to amend the Greater New York Charter in relation to the Board of Education of the City of New York (1913). BOE Pamphlet Collection, Box 1. Milbank Memorial Library.

Men teachers and shortage. (1927). BOE, Bureau of Reference, Research and Statistics, Box 53, Folder NYC M, 1918–39. Milbank Memorial Library.

Men teachers needed. (1921, May 5). *School, 32,* 612.

Ment, D. (1983). Patterns of public school segregation, 1900–1940: A comparative study of New York City, New Rochelle, and New Haven. In D. Ravitch & R. Goodenow (Eds.), *Schools in cities: Consensus and conflict in American educational history* (pp. 67–110). New York: Holmes & Meier.

Mirel, J. (1993). *The rise and fall of an urban school system: Detroit, 1907–1981.* Ann Arbor: University of Michigan Press.

Miss Zipfel sues the state. (1921, June 23). *School, 32,* 750.

Miss Zipfel's bill vetoed. (1921, May 19). *School, 32,* 650.

Moffett, M. (1929). *Social background and activities of Teachers College students.* New York: Teachers College Press.

Monro, K. M. (1916). The value of historical fiction. *The History Teachers' Magazine, 7,* 266–267.

Montgomery, D. (1979). *Workers' control in America.* New York: Cambridge University Press.

Montgomery, D. (1987). Thinking about American workers in the 1920s. *International Labor and Working Class History, 32,* 4–24.

Moore, D. D. (1981). *At home in America: Second generation New York Jews.* New York: Columbia University Press.

Morris, E. H. (1929). *Personal traits and success in teaching.* New York: Teachers College Press.

Mossman, L. C. (1924). *Changing conceptions relative to the planning of lessons.* New York: Teachers College Press.

Mossman, L. C. (1929). The elementary school principal as a supervisor—Abstract. *Addresses and Proceedings of the National Education Association, 415–419.*

Muraskin, L. D. (1981). The interests of the Teachers Union, 1913–1935. In D. Ravitch & R. K. Goodenow (Eds.), *Educating an urban people: The New York City experience* (pp. 219–230). New York: Teachers College Press.

Murphy, M. (1990). *Blackboard unions: The AFT and the NEA, 1900–1980.* Ithaca, NY: Cornell University Press.

Nasaw, D. (1985). *Children of the city.* Garden City, NY: Anchor.

Negro and the northern public schools, The. (1923). *The Crisis, 25,* 205.

New school buildings and sites. (Report of the superintendent of Schools, 1923–26). (1926). New York City: Board of Education.

New York City Board of Education. (1928). *The teacher handbook: A guide to use in the City of New York.* New York: Author.

New York training school for teachers. (1922, March 23). *School, 33,* 1.

Newhouse, V. (1989). *Wallace K. Harrison: Architect.* New York: Rizzoli.

Nifenecker, E. A. (1936). *Statistical reference data showing school background conditions, factors, trends and problems, 1900–34.* (Publication No. 28, vol 1). New York: Bureau of Reference, Research and Statistics, Board of Education of the City of New York.

Olneck, M., & Lazerson, M. (1974). The school achievement of immigrant children, 1900–30. *History of Education Quarterly, 14,* 452–482.

O'Malley, M. (1990). *Keeping watch: A History of American time.* New York: Penguin.

One teacher in ten is declared absent. (1922, May 13). *New York Times,* p. 18.

Oppenheimer, J. J. (1924). *The visiting teacher movement.* New York: Public Education Association.

Ortman, E. J. (1923). *Teacher Councils: The organized means for securing the co-operation of all workers in the school.* Montpelier: Capital City Press.

Osgood, E. L. (1916). Experimental course in industrial history. *The History Teachers' Magazine, 7,* 98–102.

O'Shea, W. J. (1924–25). *Twenty-seventh annual report of the superintendent of schools.* New York: Board of Education.

Osofsky, G. (1966). *Harlem: The making of a ghetto, Negro New York 1890–1930.* New York: Harper & Row.

Otis, E. P. (1922). America, the beautiful. *Ungraded, 7,* 140–144.

Outline for sex education in the high school, An. (1922). *School and Society, 15,* 650–652.

Owen, N. (1931). Just another day. *The Teachers' Forum, 1,* 3 (Memphis Teachers' Association, AFT Local 52).

Ozga, J., & Lawn, M. (1988). Schoolwork: Interpreting the labour process of teaching. *British Journal of Sociology of Education, 9,* 323–336.

Palmer, J. T. (1919). The importance of the teacher in the school organization. *Elementary School Journal, 19*, 541–544.

Parsons, E. D. (1920). Fallacious economy in education. *School and Society, 11*, 10–14.

Patri, A. (1925, June 25). Correspondence to Floyd Matson. Angelo Patri Papers, Box 1, Library of Congress.

Patri, A. (n.d.). Autobiography manuscript. Angelo Patri Papers, Box 83, Library of Congress.

Pauly, P. J. (1991). The development of high school biology: New York City, 1900–1925. *ISIS, 82*, 662–688.

Perlmann, J. (1985). Curriculum and tracking in the transformation of the American high school: Providence, R. I., 1880–1930. *Journal of Social History, 18*, 29–55.

Phillips, F. M. (1926–27). *A preliminary study of teacher load in elementary schools.* Washington, DC: United States Bureau of Education.

Pierce, B. L. (1926). *Public opinion and the teaching of history in the United States.* New York: Knopf.

Pine, T. (1977, September 14). Interviewed by Edith Gordon, MG 101, Special Collections. Milbank Memorial Library.

Play or death? (1926, 25 December). *The School Parent, 5*, 3.

Prentice, A., & Theobald, M. (Ed.). (1991). *Women who taught: Perspectives on the history of women and teaching.* Toronto: University of Toronto Press.

Proctor, W. M., & Brown, E. J. (1928). College admission requirements in relation to curriculum revision in secondary schools. In *The development of the high school curriculum.* Washington, DC: National Education Association, Department of Superintendence, Sixth Yearbook, 159–194.

Public address systems. (1920–29). In *The American school and university, 1928–29.* New York: American School Publishing Corp, 263.

Pulliam, R. (1930). *Extra-instructional activities of the teacher.* New York: Doubleday.

Pupils use tiny glass bombs to startle teachers. (1922, March 23). *School, 33*, 401.

Quance, F. M. (1926). *Part time types of elementary schools in New York City.* New York. Teachers College Press.

Quantz, R. (1985). The complex visions of female teachers and the failure of unionization in the 1930s: An oral history. *History of Education Quarterly, 25*, 439–458.

Quantz, R. (1992). Interpretive method in historical research: Ethnohistory reconsidered. In R. Altenbaugh (Ed.), *The teacher's voice: A social history of teaching in twentieth century America* (pp. 174–190). Bristol, UK: Falmer.

Questions and suggestions on the physical conditions of the public schools. (n.d.). UFT, Unprocessed papers, Box #1. Wagner Archives.

Raftery, J. (1988). Missing the mark: Intelligence testing in Los Angeles public schools, 1922–32. *History of Education Quarterly, 28*, 73–93.

Ravitch, D. (1988). *The great school wars: A history of the New York City public schools.* New York: Basic Books.

Raymond, A. (1931). *A study of New York's public school system.* New York: New York Herald Tribune.

Rebel song. A. (1924). *The English Journal, 13*, 674.

Reed, T. G. (1927). *Teachers' reactions to school administration.* Unpublished master's thesis, Teachers College, Columbia University, New York.

Reese, W. P. (1928). *Personality and success in teaching.* Boston: Graham.

Regan, P. A. (1974). *An historical study of the nurse's role in school health programs from 1902–1973.* Unpublished doctoral dissertation, Boston University.

Report of resignations of teachers during calendar year 1919. (1920, February 23). BOE, Bureau of Reference, Research, and Statistics, Box 54, Folder NYC Q-R. Milbank Memorial Library.

Report of the legal advisory committee. (1926). *Brooklyn Teachers Association, Fifty-Second Annual Report, 51.*

Report of the special committee on the assignment of teachers on Jewish holidays. (1929–30). *Brooklyn Teachers Association Fifty-Sixth Annual Report, 76–81.*

Report of visit to P. S. 90. (1930, January 27). UFT, Unprocessed papers, Box #1. Wagner Archives.

Report on construction and maintenance. (1924). *Twenty-sixth annual report of the superintendent of schools.* New York City: Board of Education.

Rice, J. (1969). *The public-school system of the United States.* New York: Arno Press.

Rich, S. G. (1924). Is school discipline useful? *Journal of Educational Method, 4,* 250.

Richardson, E. R. (1928). From pram to office. *Journal of the American Association of University Women, 21,* 115–118.

Rider, F. (1924). *Rider's New York City.* New York: Macmillan.

Rinehart, A. D. (1983). *Mortals in an immortal profession: An oral history of teaching.* New York: Irvington.

Rockwell, E. G. (1922, February 16). Commandments for teachers. *School, 33,* 426.

Rodgers, D. (1978). *The work ethic in industrial America, 1850–1920.* Chicago: University of Chicago Press.

Rosenthal, D. B., & Bybee, R. W. (1987). Emergence of the biology curriculum: A science of life or science of living. In T. S. Popkewitz (Ed.), *The formation of the school subjects* (pp. 123–144). New York: Falmer.

Rousmaniere, K. (1994). Losing patience and staying professional: Women teachers and the problem of classroom discipline in New York City schools in the 1920s. *History of Education Quarterly, 34,* 49–68.

Rousmaniere, K. (1996). Teachers' work and the social relations of school space in early-twentieth century North American urban schools. *Historical Studies in Education/Revue d'Histoire de L'Education, 8,* 42–64.

Rury, J. (1989). Who became teachers? The social characteristics of teaching in American history. In D. Warren (Ed.), *American teachers: Histories of a profession at work* (pp. 9–48). New York: Macmillan.

Rury, J. (1991). *Education and women's work: Female schooling and the division of labor in urban America, 1870–1930.* Albany: State University of New York Press.

Russell, J. E. (1920). Organization of teachers. *Educational Review, 60,* 129–135.

Salaries in city school systems, 1926–7. (1927). *Research Bulletin of the National Education Association, 5,* 73.

Saltzberg, F. B. (1925). A scrap of paper. *Brooklyn Teachers' Association Fifty-First Annual Report, 45.*

Salwen, P. (1989). *Upper West Side story: A history and guide.* New York: Abbeville.

Sampson, C. H. (1922). The classroom that I would have. *American School Board Journal, 67,* 61, 139.

Sampson, H. (1926). Vacation. *The English Journal, 15,* 470.

Says big classes Fordize schools. (1929, June 17). *New York Times,* p. 25.

Schlocklow, O. (1914–15). Report of the committee on school problems. *Brooklyn Teachers Association Forty-First Annual Report,* 16–28.

School heads seek to cut waste time. (1925, April 4). *New York Times,* p. 36.

School library inventory statistics, 1926–33. BOE Bureau of Libraries. Milbank Memorial Library.

School red tape repels teachers. (1920, September 11). *New York Evening Post,* p. 8.

School rest rooms. (1925). *American School Board Journal, 70,* 46, 135.

School Survey Committee. (1924). *Survey of public school system, City of New York.* New York: Board of Education of the City of New York.

Scott, A. C. (1923). Is there any consolation in this for you? *The Teachers' Bulletin of Districts 41 and 42, Long Island City, NY, 1,* 10.

Sedlak, M., & Schlossman, S. (1987). Who will teach?: Historical perspectives on the changing appeal of teaching as a profession. *Review of Research in Education, 14,* 93–131.

Shannon, J. R. (1927). *Personal and social traits requisite for high grade teaching in secondary schools.* Unpublished doctoral dissertation, Indiana University, Bloomington, Indiana.

Shulman, H. M. (1930). Crime prevention and the public schools. *Journal of Educational Sociology, 4,* 69–81.

Shulman, H. M. (1938). *Slums of New York.* New York: Albert & Charles Boni, Inc.

Simmons, E. B. (1920, June 19). Portrait of a modern girl doing things on the jump. *New York Evening Post,* p. 6.

Simon, K. (1982). *Bronx primitive: Portraits in a childhood.* New York: Harper & Row.

Sinclair, U. (1924). *The goslings: A study of American schools.* Pasadena, CA. Author.

Spradley, J. (1979). *The ethnographic interview.* New York: Holt Rinehart.

Spring, J. (1974). Mass culture and school sports. *History of Education Quarterly, 14,* 483–499.

Spring vacation. (1925). *Journal of the National Education Association, 14,* 190.

Stanic, G. M. A. (1986). The growing crisis in mathematics education in the early twentieth century. *Journal for Research in Mathematics Education, 17,* 190–205.

Steedman, C. (1985). "The mother made conscious": The historical development of a primary school pedagogy. *History Workshop, 20,* 149–163.

Stevens, E. W. (1972). Social centers, politics, and social efficiency in the Progressive Era. *History of Education Quarterly, 12,* 16–33.

Stevens, R. (1912). *The question as a measure of efficiency in instruction.* New York: Teachers College Press.

Stevenson, P. R. (1923). *Smaller classes or larger: A study of the relation of size to the efficiency of teaching.* Bloomington, IN: Public School Publishing Co.

Still, B. (1956). *Mirror for Gotham: New York as seen by contemporaries from Dutch days to the present.* New York: New York University Press.

Storey, T. A., Small, W. S., & Salisbury, E. G. (1922). *Recent State Legislation for Physical Education* (Bulletin, No 1). Washington, DC: United States Bureau of Education.

Strober, M. H., & Best, L. (1979). The female/male salary differential in public schools: Some lessons from San Francisco, 1879. *Economic Inquiry, 17,* 218–236.

Super-vision demanded in supervision, The. (1928). *Childhood Education, 4,* 312.

Survey of group of school buildings by outside organizations. (1925). *Journal of the Board of Education of the City of New York.* New York: Board of Education, 868–873.

Suzzallo, H. (1913). The reorganization of the teaching profession. *Addresses and Proceedings of the National Education Association,* 362–379.

Taggart, R. (1995). Business influence on educational reform and the forgotten teacher. *Journal of the Midwest History of Education Society, 22,* 15–27.

Taylor, J. S. (1912). Measurement of educational efficiency. *Educational Review, 44,* 350–351.

Teacher and clerk, too. (1927, August 22). *New York Times,* p. 16.

Teacher-training institutions should recruit their quotas from the nation's most promising youth. (1926). *Research Bulletin of the National Education Association, 4,* 179.

Teachers' Rest Room. (1922). BOE Photography Collection, #G1678, Milbank Memorial Library.

Teachers Council, The. (1928, November). *The Union Teacher,* 6–7.

Teachers' League of New York City, The. (1914). BOE Vertical File 711 NYC O-Z, 1919–1949, Box 108. Milbank Memorial Library.

Teachers whose services have been discontinued during the period from September 1921–November 1926. (1926). BOE, Bureau of Reference, Research, and Statistics, Box 53, Folder 1918–5. Milbank Memorial Library.

Tebbel, J. (1988). For children, with love and profit: Two decades of book publishing for children. In S. A. Jagusch (Ed.), *Stepping away from tradition: Children's books of the twenties and thirties* (pp. 13–36). Washington, DC: Library of Congress.

Temple, A. (1928). Value of supervision from the standpoint of the teacher. *Childhood Education, 4,* 315–317.

Tenenbaum, S. (1949). Brownsville's age of learning. *Commentary, 5,* 173–178.

Thrasher, F. M. (1928). How to study the boys' gang in the open. *Journal of Educational Sociology, 1,* 244–255.

Tildsley, J. L. (1920). The crisis in education. *High Points, 2,* 32–35.

Tildsley, J. L. (1932). The professional aliveness of the high school teachers of the City of New York (Annual report of the superintendent of schools, New York City Board of Education).

To fine Mrs McQuirk? (1921, May 12). *School, 32,* 631.

Tropea, J. L. (1987). Bureaucratic order and special children: Urban schools, 1890s–1940s. *History of Education Quarterly, 27,* 29–53.

Turner, P. V. (1987). *Campus: An American planning tradition.* Cambridge, MA: MIT Press.

Twenty-eighth annual report of the superintendent of schools. (1925–26). New York: Board of Education.

Two stormy years. (1916–1918). St. Paul Federation of Teachers, Box #1, Folder 1–1. Reuther Library.

Tyack, D. (1974). *The one best system.* Cambridge, MA: Harvard University Press.

Tyack, D., & Berkowitz, M. (1977). The man nobody liked: Toward a social history of the truant officer, 1840–1940. *American Quarterly, 29,* 31–54.

Tyack, D., & Cuban, L. (1995). *Tinkering toward utopia: A century of public school reform.* Cambridge: Harvard University Press.

Tyack, D., & Hansot, E. (1990). *Learning together: A history of coeducation in American public schools.* New Haven, CT: Yale University Press.

Tyack, D. B., & Strober, M. H. (1981). Jobs and gender: A history of the structuring of educational employment by sex. In P. Schmuck & W. W. Charters (Eds.), *Educational policy and management: Sex differentials* (pp. 131–152). San Diego: Academic Press.

Unionizing teachers. (1919). *American School Board Journal, 59,* 56.

United Parents Association. (1929). School lunch survey of New York City. United Parents Association Papers, Box 1. Milbank Memorial Library.

Updegraff, H. (1922). Report of the Committee on Participation of Teachers in Management. *Elementary School Journal, 22,* 783–788.

Urban, W. (1982). *Why teachers organized.* Detroit: Wayne State University Press.

Variation in school attendance. (1922, November 2). *School, 34,* 141.

Vaughan, A. O. (1928, February.). Teaching load. *National League of Teachers' Associations Bulletin, 22.*

Waller, W. (1932). *The sociology of teaching.* New York: John Wiley & Sons.

Waller, W. (1970). Notes on the transformation of the teacher. In W. J. Goode, F. Furstenberg, Jr., & L. R. Mitchell (Eds.), *Willard W. Waller on the family, education and war* (pp. 233–245). Chicago: University of Chicago Press.

Ware, C. (1965). *Greenwich Village, 1920–1930.* New York: Harper & Row.

Wattenberg, W. (1936). *On the educational front.* New York: Columbia University Press.

Weiler, K. (1989). Women's history and the history of women teachers. *Journal of Education, 171,* 9–30.

Weinberg, M. (1977). *A chance to learn: The history of race and education in the United States.* Cambridge, UK: Cambridge University Press.

Weiner, L. (1992, April). *Teacher unions and professional organization: Re-examining Margaret Haley's counsel on councils.* Paper presented at the annual meeting of the American Educational Research Association, San Francisco.

Weisz, H. R. (1968). *Irish-American and Italian-American educational views and activities, 1870–1900: A comparison.* Unpublished doctoral dissertation, Columbia University, New York.

Welty, H. O. (1930). Administration of supervision in larger high schools. *California Quarterly of Secondary Education, 5,* 181.

West of Central Park Association. (1937). A startling survey of public school conditions in the eighth school district, Manhattan. New York: School Committee of the West of Central Park Association.

What women investigators found in old city school buildings. (1921, June 18). *New York Evening Post,* p. 11.

Why teachers leave school: Results of Miss Lathrop's investigation at Washington. (1921, May 5). *School, 32,* 609.

Wickman, E. K. (1928). *Children's behavior and teachers' attitudes.* New York: Commonwealth Fund.

Wood, G. W. (1992). *Schools that work: America's most innovative public education programs.* New York: Plume.

Yezierska, A. (1975). *Bread givers.* New York: Persea.

Young, E. F. (1901). *Isolation in the schools.* Chicago: University of Chicago Press.

Young, W. H. (1919). The personality of the teacher. *Education, 39,* 374–380.

Zilversmit, A. (1993). *Changing schools: Progressive education theory and practice, 1930–60.* Chicago: University of Chicago Press.

Zinman, M. E. (1923). The value of intelligence tests. *High Points, 5,* 17.

Index

About the Author

KATE ROUSMANIERE is an assistant professor in the Department of Educational Leadership at Miami University in Oxford, Ohio. Since taking her doctorate in the history of education from Teachers College, Columbia University, in 1992, she has served as the 1995 AERA Program Chair for History and Historiography, co-edited (with Kari Dehli and Ning de Coninck-Smith) *Discipline, Moral Regulation, and Schooling: A Social History,* and published numerous journal articles.